PRAISE FOR RASHAD JENN
THE IF IN LIFE

"*The IF in Life* ... The title alone speaks volumes. As a fellow NY Giant, I've come to know Rashad as a genuine mentor. He taught me the difference between being an NFL player and a pro-athlete. His deeply missed presence in the locker room is a great testament to the incredible obstacles he has tackled to get to where he is today. This book chronicles that story, and gives you great principles for handling the IFs of life along the way! HIGHLY RECOMMENDED!"

—ODELL BECKHAM, JR.—NFL All-Pro
Wide Receiver for the NY Giants

"Although we all come from different backgrounds and have different stories, humanity has this in common: we only get one shot at this life. Rashad has written a book that will help anybody who wants to get out of "what could have been" and start making the most of the opportunities we have. I know *The IF in Life* will be a blessing to many!"

—CARL LENTZ—Hillsong NYC Pastor

"In all my seasons on *Dancing with the Stars*, I've never had a partner so committed to hard work and excellence. I know and love so much about Rashad, but this book reveals things that I could never imagine having to go through. More people need to read this and be affected by his philosophy in life. You'll fall in love with Rashad's story. And you'll be inspired to become your best self! *The IF in Life* would be a great movie someday!"

—EMMA SLATER—Dancer/Choreographer for
Dancing with the Stars, Season 24 Champion

"In *The IF in Life*, Rashad Jennings tackles the obstacles and navigates the hurdles he had to overcome to make it from a kid with a dream to an NFL team. You will be inspired, encouraged, and motivated to pursue your own dream like never before. If you love a great true story, and you need inspiration for your life, then The IF in Life is just the book for you!"

—MILES MCPHERSON—Founder and Senior Pastor, The Rock Church, San Diego; Former NFL Defensive Back; Motivational Speaker

"Rashad's tenacity and determination are infectious. *The IF in Life* is a great story for all audiences that is filled with precious principles for living and achieving your dreams. I absolutely love how Rashad's mom, dad, and brothers rallied around him in his childhood times of need. It just shows how much the loving support of a strong and committed family can do."

—BENJAMIN WATSON—NFL Tight End for the Baltimore Ravens, Super Bowl XXXIX Champion

NEW YORK TIMES BESTSELLER

THE IF IN LIFE

How to Get Off
Life's Sidelines
and Become Your
Best Self

RASHAD JENNINGS

WITH MARGOT STARBUCK

ZONDERVAN

The IF in Life
Copyright © 2018 by Rashad Jennings, LLC

Requests for information should be addressed to:
Zondervan, *3900 Sparks Dr. SE, Grand Rapids, Michigan 49546*

Hardcover ISBN 978-0-310-76596-7

Softcover ISBN 978-0-310-76595-0

Ebook ISBN 978-0-310-76587-5

Audio download ISBN 978-0-310-76569-1

Scripture quotations are taken from the Holy Bible, New International Version®, NIV®. Copyright © 1973, 1978, 1984, 2011 by Biblica, Inc.® Used by permission of Zondervan. All rights reserved worldwide. www.Zondervan.com. The "NIV" and "New International Version" are trademarks registered in the United States Patent and Trademark Office by Biblica, Inc.®

Any internet addresses (websites, blogs, etc.) and telephone numbers in this book are offered as a resource. They are not intended in any way to be or imply an endorsement by Zondervan, nor does Zondervan vouch for the content of these sites and numbers for the life of this book.

No part of this publication may be reproduced, stored in a retrieval system, or transmitted in any form or by any means—electronic, mechanical, photocopy, recording, or any other—except for brief quotations in printed reviews, without the prior permission of the publisher.

This is a work of nonfiction. The events and experiences detailed herein are all true and have been faithfully rendered as remembered by the author, to the best of his abilities. Some names and other identifying characteristics have been changed to protect the privacy of the individuals involved.

Published in association with the literary agency of WordServe Literary Group, Ltd., www.wordserveliterary.com.

Interior design: Denise Froehlich
Cover design: Ron Huizinga
Cover photography by: Meg Urbani

Printed in the United States of America

19 20 21 22 23 24 25 /LSC/ 10 9 8 7 6 5 4 3 2 1

This, my first book, is especially dedicated to my mom, Deborah Jennings, for being the rock our entire family could and can always depend on—no matter what. It is also dedicated to my dad, Albert, and my brothers, Butch and Bryan. You are each a true testament to what it means to be men willing to take the lead in their own various ways to create a great family. I also dedicate this book to that little overweight kid with glasses, asthma, a 0.6 GPA, and an impossible dream. This is for every tear you cried when people couldn't see in you what you always longed to become. You got us off the sidelines. I'm proud of you!

All of you together demonstrate the inestimable value of a family that loves God and loves each other. IF … I did not have you in my life, I could not have made it.

Educator guide available for download at

http://TheIfInLifeBook.com/

CONTENTS

FOREWORD

It is with great honor and privilege that I introduce you to the incredible life story of my friend and fellow former New York Giant, Rashad Jennings. Rashad is one of those professional athletes who stepped onto the NFL stage and never once allowed the fame and fortune to determine the level of his integrity. During his eight years in the league he showed us a clear picture of what a consummate professional who places a premium on being humble, teachable, and admirable looks like. I'm proud to know that he is a member of the Giants fraternity. I'm even prouder to know him as a friend.

But where does all of this come from? You see, people don't just wake up one day and suddenly find themselves to be people of character. The kind of hard work, faith, and integrity Rashad shows is formed over time ... over years. And that's where Rashad's story, *The IF in Life* comes in. This book reminds me of my own journey, and I have a feeling it will sound familiar to a lot of you too. Personally, I was immediately drawn to its subtitle—*How to Get Off Life's Sidelines and Become Your Best Self*—because I could not have become the person I am today if I had let difficulties I faced in life keep me sidelined.

You see, life is filled with situations and circumstances that present us with opportunities to consider that big little word—*IF*. As we live, we will be faced with decisions both big and small. This book helps us see that *if* we want to become our best self, we need to carefully consider the empirical truth that consistently making good choices is the only path to real success and enjoyment in life. The alternative to this is that one bad decision, one momentary failure to respect an "*if*" in your life, can set you back years, or perhaps even a lifetime, when it comes to your goals.

Even after having achieved so many of my own dreams, I am truly inspired by this story of a once overweight, asthmatic kid, who struggled academically. As a teenager, Rashad made the mature decision to *stop letting life happen to* him, and instead *start making life happen for* him. The man he has become is living proof of what you can do when you decide to apply yourself and let no one and nothing stop you.

Tom Coughlin, the great coach under which we both played, once said about the NFL: "*Every year that you enter this business and this game, the goal is the Super Bowl.*" While I totally agree with that as a football player, there is a Super Bowl that every person has to face—life. The good thing about life's Super Bowl is that you don't have to wait to be called off the sidelines, you can get up on your own and get after it!

I am positive that you will thoroughly enjoy *The IF in Life*—it is a great story! Being in TV myself, I would not be surprised if it's made into a movie. I am also confident that as you read Rashad's story, you will begin to imagine becoming your best self. So, prepare to be inspired to take charge of your life and play to win!

—MICHAEL STRAHAN, NFL Hall of
Fame Defensive End, NFL Analyst, and
Emmy Winning TV Personality

INTRODUCTION

When I was thirteen years old, I made a decision that guided the course of my life. At the time, I couldn't see how vowing not to smoke or drink, like my dad did, would shape my future. But a single, small choice I made that day set me on a path that would influence every second of my life from that moment on.

It's decisions like these that define our futures, and usually, the decisions aren't easy ones. Maybe you've been treated poorly, but chose to respond with dignity and respect. Faced a setback, but got back in the game and gave one-hundred percent. Were failing, but put in the hard work to succeed. Maybe you refused to listen to naysayers, choosing to chase your dreams anyway or were expected to make the same negative choices your parents did, but chose a different path instead. A single decision—the right "yes" or the right "no"— can shape the course of your life.

I recognize some of those critical points in my own journey:

"If I hadn't returned to the gridiron after a season away . . ."

"If I hadn't buckled down to improve my grades and my health . . ."

"If I'd gotten angry and ugly when a friend's father disrespected me . . ."

"If I'd given up when others didn't believe in me . . ."

"If I'd patterned my life after my dad's . . ."

The *if* in life refers to those formative choices that shape your future. These decisions you're making today are the ones that will determine *if* you'll experience the life God has for you.

The good news is that the *if* is up to you.

And, trust me, there will be plenty of people who will have opinions about your future. Some might make predictions like, "You'll never . . ." or "You can't . . ." or "You won't . . ." And *if* you listen to them, it's true: *you won't.*

But if you tip your ear toward the voice that whispers, "You can do it . . ." and "I got you . . ." and "I believe in you," you'll experience the good plan God has for your life.

When I was a teenager, I recognized that holy voice. It sounded a lot like some of the encouraging voices I already knew: my mother's, my brothers', and that one teacher who said, "Rashad, I know you are going to achieve whatever you put your mind to. I know you are going to be successful." That is the voice to trust.

People will lift you up or push you down, but what you do with the *if* in life is up to you.

Rashad Jennings

CHAPTER 1

THE DREAMER

On the night I was born, my dad and one of his buddies were watching football. When it was time to choose a name for his third son, Dad decided to name me after All-American running back, and later wide receiver, Ahmad Rashad. At first, my mom thought that was foolishness, but when she discovered that Rashad means "thinker" and "counselor" she agreed.

I haven't always been a thinker or a counselor—those qualities came along as I grew older—but I've always loved football. Long before I knew the origin of my own name, I dreamed of being out on that field. So it was no surprise that as soon as I was old enough to play, I followed in my namesake's footsteps.

I was six years old the first time Mom took me to Jump Park to play peewee football with the town rec league. Being the size I was, and because the league was organized by weight and not by age, I was bumped up to a team with boys who were as old as eight or nine.

As I waved good-bye to buddies my age and walked across the field to join the older guys, I felt nervous and excited. Two sentences ping-ponged in my mind:

Oh, man, I gotta play with the older guys.

Oh, man, I get to play with the older guys.

I'd been eagerly awaiting this day. As far as I was concerned, there was no better position than a running back. These were undeniably the fiercest guys on the field: relentless, resilient athletes with unbelievable endurance. They ran through defenders like steam locomotives, and when they went down, they fell onto the turf like ballerinas. They were quick and agile. They had great peripheral vision and could see where the holes were in the defense. (This was really important, since at any given time there are eleven people trying to kill them.) They were hard to tackle because they had a good center of gravity. They were illusionists who could mislead the defense, quickly cutting in a different direction. And, whether they liked it or not, they were able to take a beating.

As a kid, I possessed very few of these qualities. I wore glasses that would slide down my nose when I got sweaty. I was heavy, so when I hit the ground, I hit hard. I tired easily, sometimes struggling to breathe. And yet none of those things caused me to doubt that I could achieve my dream. I'd been watching football my whole life. My big brothers both played football. Butch wore blue and white for E.C. Glass High School. I don't remember many of his games, because he was fourteen years older than me. Bryan was in high school when I first started playing football, and he rocked red and black for Jefferson Forest High School. And we'd all watch NFL games on Sunday afternoons in our living room with Dad, my cousins, aunts, and uncles.

I was confident on that first day of peewee league because I already saw myself as a successful running back. When Bryan played for Jefferson Forest, I'd run around the sidelines playing football with the other players' little brothers and sisters. With every pass, handoff, or run, I imagined I was out there on the field like the Cavaliers I idolized. In my imagination, I wasn't just running the ball for Jefferson Forest High—I was running it for my beloved Arizona Cardinals, who also wore those iconic red and black colors.

So when coach blew his whistle to gather the team together, I focused my attention on him. He instructed us to go stand by the volunteers who'd be coaching the various positions. Offensive linemen would meet at the fifty-yard line. Quarterbacks would meet at the twenty-yard line. Running backs would meet on the forty-yard line. And so on.

"All right," the coach instructed, "go meet your coaches."

Wearing a bucket helmet with a mouthpiece that was too big, I marched straight to the coach who'd be working with the running backs.

The coach took one look at me and said, "Hey, man, I think you're in the wrong place. The offensive linemen are over there."

He pointed toward the center of the field.

But I would not be dismissed so easily. When I'd pause to catch my breath on the sidelines of Jefferson Forest games, I'd watch the players who ran the ball down the field, darting past the defense and dodging tackles. I could see myself weaving past defenders, taking gazelle-like strides into the end zone, where I'd humbly look to the heavens to thank God for victory. I'd studied greats like Emmitt Smith, Eddie George, and Curtis Martin. When I watched them move down the field, I could see myself in their cleats. I had a very clear sense that I was destined to play running back, and no one was going to keep me from realizing the vision I had for my future.

As all the boys sorted themselves out, I started to argue with the coach.

"I wanna play for you," I told him.

He paused to choose his words carefully.

"I think you're going to be a great offensive lineman. Why don't you try that today?"

Feeling confused, I shook my head.

"What's your name?" he asked.

Frustrated, I mumbled, "Rashad."

Calling out to the offensive line coach, he hollered, "Hey, Cliff, can Rashad work with you?"

Cliff took one look at me and flagged me over. *Why wasn't anyone listening to me?*

"Come on over here, little man," he called, sounding happy to have me.

Grudgingly, I headed over to his squad of offensive lineman. As far as I was concerned, their jobs were boring. I knew that all they got to do was block for the runner. I did what I was told, but muttered under my breath, "This isn't over."

I spent the practice learning to engage an opponent. It felt more like sumo wrestling than football. And when we were finally released from practice, I stomped over to our car, where Mom was patiently waiting for me behind the wheel, eager to hear about my first practice.

Mom, smiling from ear to ear, asked me, "How was practice?"

Brow furrowed, I slumped into the backseat and buckled my seatbelt. "I didn't like it."

She looked surprised.

"Really?" she asked. "Why not, baby?"

She pulled out of the dusty parking lot and onto the main road, and I kept myself from looking back at the football field.

I reported, as if I was tattling on one of my big brothers, "I didn't like my position."

She nodded her head as she listened. "And why didn't you like it, Shad?"

"Because I don't wanna be an offensive lineman," I answered.

"What position do you want to play?" she asked.

"I want to be a running back!"

I sulked in silence the rest of the ride home. As we rumbled up our long gravel driveway, I continued to fume, my frustration rising with each step I climbed to our split-level home on Cimarron Road. I pulled open the door that we always left unlocked because our residential neighborhood was so safe, wishing I could slam it behind me.

My dad and Bryan were in the kitchen when I walked in,

and I launched into an angry diatribe about how unfairly I'd been treated. Finally, Dad had heard enough.

"Boy, just play offensive line!"

Really? My own dad wasn't going to take my side? It felt like the whole world was against me.

Persistence

Every practice, I'd badger the coaches to let me play running back. Finally, they put me at fullback to keep me quiet.

I heard one coach mutter under his breath, "Let him block from the backfield and he'll be all right." It worked for about one practice.

I continued to press, my six-year-old self utterly determined to follow this dream. After several weeks, when I finally wore the coaches down, they let me practice with the running backs. But it seemed like the concession was made only to shut me up. I never got the ball, and the other kids got far more attention when it came to training. Even then, I knew I didn't fit the mold for an ideal running back—at least not on the outside. But inside, it was all I wanted.

Daily, I'd remind the coaches, "I wanna run the ball."

As if they could have forgotten from the previous day's request. My pestering went on day after day, practice after practice. I didn't let up the entire season. Or the next. Or the next. And yet my coaches still refused to play me.

As a kid built for blocking, it would have been easy enough to resign myself to being an offensive lineman. At least I'd have been out there on the field! I also could have been less hardheaded about insisting that the coach play me at running back. I could have accepted the position I'd been assigned or refrained from daily announcing my resistance. But *if* I'd done either one—this was one of those first *if* decisions for me—my life would have unfolded very differently than it has. At the time, I know I just seemed like I was being kind of obnoxious. But it's because I knew what I was capable of, and I was hanging on to my dream for dear life.

Trying Something New

Although football was my passion, I have always been interested in trying new things, like learning to play an instrument, going out for a new sport, or trying a new hobby.

Toward the end of each peewee football season, Mom and I would start to see kids gathering at Jump Park to begin baseball season. I never paid them much attention, I was so focused on my own sport. But at the end of my fourth season of peewee, when I was about nine, Mom asked, "Shad, do you wanna try baseball?"

I'd never played baseball, or even *watched* baseball. But since it had the word "ball" in it, I was game.

"Sure," I answered. "What is it?"

Mom explained the basics of the game to me, but I now know it probably would have been better to have watched a game before playing one. And because my football team had gone to the finals and become league champs, I was two weeks late joining the baseball team.

My first day, my new baseball team had a game.

I showed up in an old pair of Butch's baseball pants that were too tight, with a mitt of my dad's that Mom had found for me. After introducing myself to the coach, I threw on the black shirt and hat he gave me. Then I tossed a ball back and forth with my friend Mark during warm-ups.

When the coach called us in, we gathered around him for instructions. Some kid handed me a bag of sunflower seeds, and as I looked around I could see that other kids were eating them. Putting a seed in my mouth, and passing the bag to the next guy, I thought, *This is a weird sport.*

The coach had a clipboard and began scribbling down a lineup as he announced it to us players. Probably pegging me as a power hitter because of my size, he said, "Rashad, you can bat fourth."

I had no idea what was going on, or what batting fourth even meant, but I was happy to be outside playing.

The first batter hit the ball, ran to the base to the right of home plate, and stayed there.

The second batter swung and missed once before hitting the ball right to the pitcher and running toward first base. The pitcher threw the ball to first, before the runner arrived, and the umpire hollered that he was out. I didn't understand all the rules yet, but I suspected that "out" was bad. My hunch was confirmed when I saw my teammate walk back to the dugout looking defeated.

Mark was up third. First pitch, he swung and missed. Second pitch, he swung and missed. He didn't swing at the third pitch, which looked a little high to me, anyway.

When Mark hit the fourth pitch, he ran to the base the first batter had run toward, but was tagged out before he got there. Like the player before him, I watched Mark mope as he dragged himself back to the bench.

"Rashad, you're up," my coach yelled to me.

I'd already put on one of the plastic helmets that spilled out of the equipment bag and chosen a bat. Not eager to meet the same fate as Mark, I wanted to get some clarity on my marching orders.

"Coach," I asked, "you want me to hit the ball and run to that base?"

"No," he clarified. "I want you to hit the ball and run to *all* the bases."

Filing away my instructions, I stepped up to the batter's box and waited for the pitch. The first pitch hit the dirt before bouncing over the plate, but I swung anyway. I missed.

"Stee-rike!" the umpire announced.

The second pitch sailed over the plate, but I swung and missed again.

Each miss only fueled my resolve to make contact and send the ball flying.

I pushed my glasses up my nose. Then, holding my bat the way I'd seen the first three batters do, I waited for the next pitch. As the pitch whizzed toward the plate, I swung with all my might and felt the crack of the bat against the ball. Hands stinging, I saw the ball soar past the infield and fly into the grassy area beyond.

Dropping my bat, I took off running—straight to third base. I'd seen what happened at first base, and I didn't want any part of it. So I ran to third, tagged it, and started running right back to home plate.

The center fielder had relayed the ball to the short stop, who had no idea what to do with it. The crowd was also befuddled. If I'd been a younger kid, they probably would have started waving and shouting for me to run to first. But I was nine, old enough to know better, and they couldn't figure out what I was doing. After thinking it over, the short stop threw the ball to the pitcher, who threw it to the catcher.

Too late! I'd already tagged home plate. I was high-fiving some of my friends when the coach started yelling at me. I tried to high-five the coach, but he wasn't having it.

"What was that?!" he demanded.

Glancing at the faces around me, I couldn't figure out why everyone else wasn't as excited as I was.

"What are you talking about, Coach? I scored!"

He remained unimpressed.

"Shad, what were you doing out there?" he asked again.

I calmly explained, "Two other guys got out at first, so I went to third."

I'd thought it was a pretty smart strategy. My coach did not.

That was my first and last season of baseball, though I learned a very important lesson: there are no shortcuts. If I was going to accomplish anything—especially my dream of being a running back—I was going to have to do it the hard way. I wouldn't succeed at every practice or every game, but I had to keep running to first base or else I'd never make it home.

◆ ◆ ◆

A few months after my ill-fated baseball season, while Mom was doing errands, another activity caught my attention. When we got out of the car I looked in the window of a local dance studio. A class of kids my age were dancing in rhythmic step with one another.

"What's that?" I asked Mom.

"Come on, Shad." She hurried me along, focused on her to-do list. "Let's go. That's called tap dancing."

I was captivated, and I continued thinking about those bouncy kids throughout the day.

That evening, Mom called Dad and me to the dinner table. As always, my mom asked about my day, what I'd learned and what I'd done, but Dad stayed silent, focused on his meal. When I was young, he never took much of an interest in what I was doing. I was so hungry for a good word from him—"Great job, Rashad," or "I'm proud of you," or "I love you"—but those words never came.

After we prayed, and started eating, I announced, "I want to tap dance."

Dad just about spit his mouthful of food.

"What?" he asked, shocked.

Mom explained, "Today, when we went to the post office, Shad saw a tap dance class."

I'd been intrigued by the performance I'd seen. And while other boys I knew might have thought dancing was too "girly," it never crossed my mind. It just looked fun to me. But activities cost money. And although we had everything we needed, we didn't have extra money for dance classes. Both of my parents tried to dissuade me, but I kept begging to take tap.

Finally, Dad came up with a plan that appeased me.

"Let's just get him some taps," he suggested, "and put them on his church shoes."

That worked for me.

A few weeks later, when the clickety clack of my Sunday shoes was still new, I was begging Mom to take *ballet* lessons. I'd heard that it was a great way to improve the balance I needed as a running back. I was still chasing that dream, even if it meant exchanging my cleats for toe shoes. Whatever I could do to get better for next season, I'd do it.

"Shad, are you sure?" Mom asked.

"Yes," I insisted. "It'll help me with football."

I could tell by the tone of her voice she wasn't convinced.

"Well," she hedged, "I'll think about it."

A few days later, she was flipping through television channels and saw the Nutcracker ballet was playing on PBS. She'd always been interested in both dance and the theater, but as the oldest of nine children, she'd spent her time caring for younger siblings. She paused to watch the graceful dance unfolding on the screen.

Remembering my insistent pleas, she asked, "So this is what you want to do, Shad?"

I'd been busy playing with a remote-control racecar, and looked up at the television.

"Wait," I demanded. "What are they wearing?"

Mom patiently explained, "Ballet dancers wear tights and leotards when they dance."

"Really?!" I asked.

She confirmed it.

Quicker than you could plié or jeté, ballet lost all appeal.

"Nah," I confirmed. "I'm out."

And that was the end of my dance aspirations, at least for the next twenty-one years.

Big Dreams

One of my favorite memories from childhood was "betting" on football with my dad. He never rooted for one particular team, but instead typically cheered for the frontrunner. I'd bet on whatever team was playing Dad's team, but we had an understanding that if the Arizona Cardinals were playing, I'd *always* have them. I loved the red and black because those were the colors we played in at Jefferson Forest High. There was also a particular player I was enamored with who played for another team. He was #32, Jamal Anderson of the Atlanta Falcons. I just loved to imitate him when he did his famous "dirty bird" celebration dance in the end zone after making a touchdown. Funny thing is, both teams had "bird" mascots, and both teams wore the same colors. So for the longest time, whenever my Cardinals scored, I'd do the "dirty bird" all around my living room. I actually believed he played for my Cardinals. I wonder why nobody ever told me that Anderson was a Falcon. Maybe they got a kick out of it, or maybe they just didn't want to bust my bubble. One thing's for sure, when I was moving my feet and flapping my wings, I could see *myself* in the Cardinals' end zone, celebrating my own touchdown.

So anyway, Dad and I would make these fake bets on every game and I would carefully record it in a log that contained a running total of our wagers. To date, I'm waiting for him to pay me the 1.2 million dollars he owes me from those bets.

Those silly bets were a lot like the dreams I had for my life back in the day. They were big! I'll be straight with you: I knew I didn't have the kind of physique, speed, lungs, or vision that would make me likely to be successful as a running back. I knew I didn't have the natural skill and gifts that others, like my brother Bryan, had been given. But I had two things some folks don't: big dreams and determination.

◆ ◆ ◆

Maybe you have big dreams for your life. I hope you do! Perhaps, like me, you want to achieve athletic success. Or maybe you want to excel in school so that you can go to college and score your dream job. Maybe you see yourself on a Broadway stage, or selling out a concert venue, or receiving an Academy Award for film editing. If you close your eyes and glimpse that moment of future success, I want you to hold on to that dream.

But maybe you're like a lot of kids who face challenges. Maybe you haven't dared to let yourself dream. Perhaps the challenges you've faced have kept you from dreaming. For instance, if no one in your family has ever gone to college, you may be afraid to claim that dream. I get that. Or you want to be a doctor, but don't know how you'd ever pay for your education, it might feel easier to not dream at all. If you struggle to read, you might be afraid to dream of high school graduation. If that's you—if you don't have a dream for your life because you're afraid to hope for what seems out of reach—I am giving you permission to dream. Yes, there will be challenges along the way. It will take commitment, hard work, and endurance to achieve your dream. But no matter how big the challenges seem today, I can assure you they will not have the final word on who you become. God made you to flourish, and God's Spirit gives you glimpses of the good that he has in store for you.

Whatever the equivalent of the "dirty bird" celebration dance is for you, I want you to do it! Visualize yourself succeeding, hold on to your dream, and trust that no obstacle is too big for you.

CHAPTER 2

MAKING PROMISES

The gray speckled horse from across the back fence eyed me as I struggled to breathe. His grassy meadow bumped up against the long row of yards behind our house that, on any given day, became our kickball diamond, baseball field, or football gridiron.

I'd been playing frisbee with my crew from the neighborhood when I began to wheeze. It wasn't unusual for me to get winded while playing at recess or with the guys on Cimarron Road. In fact, ever since kindergarten I'd had trouble breathing when I was active, or if it was really cold or hot outside. I assumed it was because I was a heavy kid and running just took more effort.

But this day was different. I'd ignored the symptoms because I was having so much fun with my friends. But when my breathing didn't improve, I went inside to see if rest and cooler air would help. Still wrestling for every breath, though, I began to feel scared. It felt like I was suffocating and that I soon wouldn't be able to breathe at all. *Why hadn't I come in sooner?*

When I heard Mom's car in the driveway, I knew help was on the way. She walked in the front door and climbed the stairs, where she found me on the couch. I just pointed at my chest, struggling to suck in air.

Without hesitating, she said, "Baby, get in the car. We're going to the doctor."

Twenty minutes later, we arrived at Dr. Morris' office. The moment we walked inside, a nurse who was standing near the check-in desk took one look at me and asked my mom what was wrong.

"He can't breathe," she reported. Even though she tried to hide it, I heard the fear in her voice.

"Do you know how to get to the hospital?" the nurse asked. "Take him right now. Don't wait for the doctor. He'd tell you to go to the hospital too."

I heard Mom praying to Jesus as she drove to the hospital, asking him to protect me.

We rushed into the emergency room of Lynchburg General Hospital. At this point, I couldn't catch my breath enough to speak. The clerk looked me up and down to decide how serious my condition was, her face pinched as she took in my symptoms.

"Can you breathe, sweetie?" the woman asked.

I shook my head no. I'd always been able to recover before, but this time I felt like someone was holding a pillow over my face. Sweat was pouring down my forehead, even though the hospital was air conditioned.

She didn't waste any time. She called a nurse, and we were

ushered right into an exam room where she clamped my finger with something she said would measure the oxygen in my blood. Mom held my other hand, the way she always did when I was sick. Then the nurse listened to my breathing with a stethoscope, first on my chest and then on my back.

"Let's get you some oxygen," she said, as if she were offering me an ice cream cone. I was only ten, but even I knew that getting oxygen wasn't optional. I continued to try to suck in air, with no success. I started to wonder how long I could go without breathing properly, and even Mom started to seem panicked, losing the calm façade she'd maintained since she'd found me at home. It was as if the nurse's calm demeanor made room for Mom to finally express the fear she'd been hiding for my benefit.

The nurse left the room and came back with some kind of machine. She put a clear plastic mask on my face and attached it to the machine which was producing a steamy gas.

"Your airway is swollen shut," she explained, "and this should open it back up. I want you to leave this on. You good with that?"

Anxious, I nodded yes.

She watched me expectantly, waiting for me to give her a signal that I was improving. Only I wasn't. She checked the clamp on my finger, and didn't look like she liked what she saw.

The nurse said to my mother, "I'm going to get the doctor. We're probably going to need to sedate him and intubate him."

She hurried out of the room.

My mother rubbed my back and assured me, "You got this, baby. You're gonna be just fine."

I wanted to believe her, but I was terrified.

A tall doctor with gray hair rushed in, his white lab coat like a cape behind him.

"Hey, buddy," he said, "how you doing?"

Taught to be respectful by my mother, I opened my mouth, but wasn't able to make a sound.

He kept talking, as he checked me over. "I want to put a tube down your throat to help you breathe. And since that's not always fun, Kathy is going to give you a shot that's going to help you relax . . ."

Before I could worry about the shot, it was over. Sounds became distant and I felt myself drifting away. The last thing I remember seeing was the worry on Mom's face, and the last sounds I heard were her fierce prayers for God to help me.

Finally, Answers

When I woke up, Mom was still by my side.

"Hey, baby," she said, with her sweet smile.

When I tried to speak, I felt a mask taped to my face and realized there was a tube down my throat. Feeling sort of freaked out by the sensation, I looked to Mom for reassurance.

"Don't try to talk," she coached me. "You breathing okay?"

I gave her a thumbs-up. And despite how weird it felt to have the tube in my airway, I was no longer gasping for breath.

"If the doctor says you're doing all right, we can go home tonight," she explained. "But you'll need to stay in bed for a while at home."

The doctor came to check on me a few minutes later. I wanted to ask him what had gone wrong—how had this happened to me? Was it permanent? Why couldn't I breathe on my own? But all I could do was wait for him to give me the answers I wanted.

"You doing better?" he asked.

I nodded yes.

The doctor explained, "You've got something called asthma. Have you heard of that before?"

I shrugged my shoulders, poked out my lip, and looked up to the sky like a weird emoji. I'd heard the word, but I didn't know what it meant.

He continued, "You know how sometimes when you're running it feels hard to breathe?"

Had my mom told him that?

I nodded again.

"When your lungs work hard, they can become swollen, making it hard to breathe."

I understood what he was saying. I hadn't been out of breath because I was fat—I was sick. I wasn't sure which was worse.

"And what happened to you today was called an asthma attack. The good news is, we can give you some medicine to help you feel better, and I'm going to give your mom a list of foods that will be good for you."

That didn't sound fun. Not if vanilla-chocolate swirl ice cream wasn't on the list. Which I suspected it wasn't.

"Do you have a pet at home?" he asked my mom.

Now I really didn't like where this was headed.

"We are taking care of my oldest son's dog right now, a mutt he got from the pound."

No! I don't want to lose Princess.

"I hate to say this," the doctor said, "but no pets."

No pets?! My situation kept getting worse instead of better. And if we had to get rid of Butch's cocker spaniel-mix, it was going to be all my fault.

Then he turned to me, explaining, "I want you to be active, doing things like walking, swimming, or biking. But I don't want you playing team sports."

If I could have screamed, I would have. My eyes flew open wide and I looked to Mom to tell that doctor what was what.

"That isn't going to be easy for Rashad," she said hesitantly. "He loves football."

I shot her a look as if to say, *Not easy?! That man just gave me a death sentence!*

The doctor thought about this. "I'll make sure his pediatrician gets our report, and he can keep an eye on it. But it is possible he could have another attack if he overexerts himself. You'll have to be careful."

I prayed that my pediatrician—who knew football was my life—would understand the seriousness of the situation. I *had* to play football.

No matter what.

Living with Asthma

I had mixed feelings about being diagnosed with asthma. I hated that I had this new label that meant *sick*. But I also felt relieved, knowing that there was a reason I'd been suffering. When I'd reported to my gym teachers how much I struggled on the mile run, they'd always treated me like I was lazy or out of shape. Yes, I was big, but I wasn't lazy. Now the doctor's diagnosis legitimized my symptoms.

I began taking an inhaler with me everywhere I went, but kids teased me whenever I had to use it. So as often as I could, I kept it hidden away in my backpack. If I had to use it, I'd be as discreet as possible, dipping into the bathroom or even trying to bend into my locker so no one would see. I also started to recognize what weather conditions and which activities were most likely to trigger an attack.

Mom learned everything she could about asthma and was my superhero protector. If she was taking me and a friend to a restaurant, a mall, or a movie theater, she'd park first and instruct us, "Stay in the car. I'm going to check and see if anyone's smoking." That was back in the day when smoking was allowed in most places. If a public place was filled with smoke, we'd keep going.

What was more unwieldy than public smoking, which we could choose to avoid, was smoking under our own roof. Most of my early childhood memories feature my dad with a cigarette in one hand and a drink in the other.

In his youth, Dad had been a very gifted athlete—he'd

played football, basketball, and baseball for E. C. Glass High School, where Butch had also attended. In fact, Dad earned a full scholarship to Nebraska University to play defensive end for the Huskers. But my parents, who'd been high school sweethearts, started their family early. So instead of heading off to college—as the first in his family who would have done so—my father joined the Air Force to earn money to support his young family. He served in Japan prior to being discharged with a disability before I was born. The years he spent in the service hadn't been kind to him, and he suffered some difficult days in the aftermath.

Because Butch was fourteen years older than me, and Bryan ten years older than me, their experiences with our father were very different from mine. They remembered a tall, strong leader who was the kind of father every boy dreams of. He playfully rough-housed with them when they were small. He showed up to support them at their little league games. He was actively involved in parenting. But after he retired, Dad became someone very different. He began smoking and drinking and, as a result, the father I now experienced was a shrunken version of the one they'd known and loved.

At first, after my diagnosis, Dad smoked outside our home, instead of inside. He'd wander out after dinner, or before dinner, to light up. But after a few months, he was smoking in the house again.

One day when I was thirteen, while Mom was still at her job at a local radio station, I was downstairs after school when I smelled smoke wafting through the vents. Dad knew the doctor had warned me not to be around smoke, and yet he continued to smoke when I was near. It seemed to me like his cigarettes and alcohol were more important to him than I was.

I'd had enough.

I grabbed a T-shirt from my drawer and walked upstairs toward my parents' bedroom. Pressing the shirt against my mouth and nose, I opened the door to Dad's room and tentatively stepped inside. My heart raced as I considered confronting my father.

I asked Dad the question that had been burning in my heart for years. "Can you stop smoking and drinking? If not for yourself, then for me?"

No kid wants to say that to his dad. I knew there was a chance I'd make him mad, and what kid wants to jeopardize their relationship with their father? Part of me also feared that I'd discover that cigarettes and alcohol were more important to my dad than I was. I had no idea how he'd respond, but I felt like I had no choice.

Dad took a swig of his drink as he considered my request. Watching the routine gesture I'd seen a thousand other times made my stomach clench. After he thought for a moment, he posed a question back.

"Rashad," he asked, "what do you want to be when you get older?"

I perked up, though I felt a little confused by his interest. Dad had never before asked me what I wanted to do when I grew up. For years I'd hungered for him to take that kind of interest in me, and it was finally happening. Even though the cigarette was still burning in his hand, I didn't hesitate to answer. At thirteen, I knew exactly what I wanted for my life.

"I wanna play running back in the NFL."

Dad took a puff of his cigarette. As his face turned sour, I recognized the anger I'd grown up knowing to fear.

"Rashad," he challenged me, "you honestly think you can make it to the NFL without drinking and smoking yo'self?"

I stepped back, feeling like he'd punched me in the gut. For that brief moment I'd imagined that he wanted to know me, to hear my hopes and dreams. But he was only interested in cutting me down so that I'd feel as low as he did. Clouded by the pain and misery in his own life, he couldn't see me for who I was.

My hurt quickly gave way to anger. I refused to receive what felt like a curse from my father.

Voice trembling, lungs burning, I told him, "Dad, just to prove you wrong, I'm never gonna do it. I'm never gonna drink or smoke a day in my life."

I turned abruptly and left, closing his door more loudly than I should have, and went outside to breathe the fresh air my lungs were craving. My body relaxed, but my mind couldn't. My father wasn't a bad man, but I didn't want to be like him, using substances as a crutch to get through the day. I was old enough to know how hard it would be to stay away from alcohol my whole life—kids I knew at school were already drinking. But I was stubborn and determined, and most of all, I wanted my father to know I could do better than him.

Making that vow to be different than my dad, when I was thirteen, was one of those critical *if* moments for me. Maybe my biggest. Although my outburst was driven by pain and anger, it turned out to be a decision that saved my life. It doesn't make any sense, but there are people with asthma who risk their health by smoking, and research shows that children of alcoholics are four times more likely than others to develop alcoholism. If I had let the statistics or my father's low opinion of me define me, I wouldn't have achieved what I have. That "if" moment made it possible.

I still believe that the promise I made that day saved my life. Little did I know that years later it would also save Dad's life.

Meeting a Hero

In addition to my dream of one day playing in the NFL, I also wanted to grow up to be a guy people could count on. For me, that meant choosing not to smoke or drink. I longed to be the kind of person my own future son or daughter would respect, the way I admired Butch and Bryan. As an athlete, I wanted to be the kind of player kids would look up to and adult fans would admire.

The first time I got to see a live NFL game, I was fourteen years old. My big brother Bryan was playing tight end for the Tennessee Oilers, and Mom and I drove ten and a half hours to the Liberty Bowl Memorial Stadium in Memphis to see him play. I was thrilled.

Throughout the game, I kept my eye on number 27, running back Eddie George. In 1996, George had been drafted in the first round of the NFL draft. At 6'3" and 235 pounds, he was a larger running back, which captured my attention. After the game, I was determined to meet him. As the team was heading toward the locker room, I ran up and thrust my program and a pen in his face.

"Can I have your autograph?" I begged.

"Sure, kid," he agreed, taking my pen and signing my program.

Then Eddie George dipped into the tunnel along with the other players. When Bryan walked by, he gave me a high five. I could not remember a happier moment.

Eddie George was living the dream. When I looked at him I could see the life I wanted for myself. I made a mental note that when I made it big, I'd pause to give kids my autograph too.

Making a Point

Despite the fact that I still believed I would play in the NFL one day, I decided to take a break from football in the tenth grade. I was tired of not playing. I was tired of hearing people tell me I was too fat and too slow. So I decided to take the season off from playing football to get myself in shape. I had a plan: work out, get stronger and leaner, and come back for junior year a totally new player, one who the coaches wanted in the starting line-up.

But that didn't happen.

While I was sincere about wanting to get in shape, I had no idea what I was doing. I didn't know the best kinds of foods to eat. I didn't know how to lift. And cardio? I still took an inhaler with me everywhere I went. If I *ever* did cardio, it was by accident, like when I was late for the school bus.

By this time, Bryan had graduated from Virginia Tech and played two years in the league, as a tight end, for the New England Patriots, the Tennessee Oilers, and the San Diego Chargers. Butch had graduated from Liberty University and had been in training camp as a fullback with the New York Giants until he experienced an injury. Upon rehabbing, he went on to play a year in the arena football league with the Milwaukee Mustangs. They were both amazing role models for me, as players and as men. When I told them I was going to take a break from football to work on my fitness, they both supported my decision.

Although my dad didn't seem to notice I wasn't playing that year, Mom loved it. She was always secretly—sometimes not so secretly—concerned one of us would get hurt, and she didn't really want any of her sons playing football. But knowing how much we loved sports, she encouraged us to try others.

"Baby, go on, play tennis," she'd encourage me.

"Shad," she once suggested, "what about golf?"

"Why don't you try out for the basketball team?" she asked.

In tenth grade, while my friends on the football team

were finishing their season, I finally took her advice. I decided to try out for the basketball team, despite the fact that I'd only played hoops in the neighborhood with friends, and never on an organized team.

The reason? My friends who played basketball for Jefferson Forest had been talking trash, saying that I couldn't make the team. And that really lit my fire. If there was one way to get me to do something, it was by telling me I couldn't. Ever since that first day of peewee, when the coach wouldn't let me be a running back, I'd become the kid who wanted to do the impossible, even if it was just to prove everyone wrong.

I showed up every day of basketball tryouts and gave it my all.

When the coach posted a list outside the gym, displaying the names of the guys who'd made the team, I was proud to find my name on it.

And then I quit the team.

Sounds crazy, right? Why go through all that effort if I wasn't going to play? I hadn't tried out for the team that year because I wanted to play basketball. I tried out for the team because my friends said I couldn't actually make the team. I wasn't about to let them, or anyone else, dissuade me from being whoever I decided to be.

I didn't know it then, but that was my first step toward growing up into the man I am today. Not a quitter—though the basketball coach definitely wasn't happy with my stunt—but someone who won't listen when the world is telling me "you can't." My friends didn't think I could make the basketball team. My dad didn't believe I could move into adulthood sober, clean, and tobacco-free. But I refused to let the negativity of others keep me from becoming who God made me to be.

◆ ◆ ◆

I suspect that you'll face obstacles in your life that might be similar to mine, or they might be very different from the ones I faced. Maybe you live with a physical or intellectual challenge. Maybe you've been labeled as the class clown and people don't expect much from you at all. Or maybe people in your family or community expect you to follow in the footsteps of a dad who abused alcohol or an uncle who went to prison.

The negativity you face does not determine who you'll become. That doesn't mean it's easy to ignore the naysayers. It's not. But rising above the attitudes and opinions of others is possible. In fact, I'm convinced that you already have what it takes to overcome the obstacles around you. When you decide that nothing can stop you, when you vow to live well and take the steps to do it, you can achieve your dreams.

CHAPTER 3

ASK QUESTIONS

School had always been a challenge for me, and in middle school I was diagnosed with a learning disorder that made it difficult for me to read. On one hand, understanding what was going on came as a relief, just as it had been when I was finally diagnosed with asthma. The school counselor explained that it didn't mean I wasn't intelligent, just that my brain processed written words differently than a lot of other students. On the other hand, it still made learning a huge challenge for me. And because I wasn't offered extra support to learn strategies to succeed, I continued to struggle academically, receiving low grades in my classes—mostly Ds and Fs. I'd try to hide my deficit from others, leaning on my winning smile and goofy, playful attitude. But inside I secretly believed I wasn't as smart or worthy as other kids. I felt ashamed.

Of course, I wasn't about to let anyone know that I felt like I wasn't smart. So I kept acting like I had it all together. Even in my classes with teachers who *knew* I didn't have it all together. I didn't want anyone to see me fail.

Expert Source

When Miss Hudson gave our tenth grade English class an assignment to write an essay on a hero, I chose to write about Dr. Martin Luther King, Jr.

When the dismissal bell rang at 3:20, I went to the school library to look up information for my report. While there was a lot of information available in books, encyclopedias, and journals, it was hard for me to wade through it all. Because I was diagnosed with a reading comprehension deficit, reading a lot of words on a page felt almost impossible to me. I knew what I wanted to say in my essay, but I struggled to put the words on paper, and to find sources to support my points.

Some people in this situation might choose to skip the assignment. Someone else might do the assignment but fudge on their sources, even fabricating them. I'm proud to say I opted against both of those. Instead, I wrote down my thoughts about Dr. King's legacy. But rather than quoting learned historians *or* making up fake quotes, I got the bright idea to quote myself. Excited by the amazing quotes I came up with, I was careful to cite my source . . . each footnote read "Rashad Jennings' Mind."

When Miss Hudson returned our papers, I was eager to see my grade. I had failed every English class I took in high school up to that point, but I felt pretty good about what I produced for that particular essay.

Miss Hudson walked past my desk and laid the paper face down in front of me.

Eager, I flipped it over, excited to see my grade. I was crushed to see a bright red "F+" with three lines below it in the top right corner of the paper. I was truly shocked—I'd put a lot of thought into that paper and had hoped to be rewarded for my effort. After simmering silently through the rest of class, I rushed to Miss Hudson's desk when the bell rang to dismiss us for lunch.

"Miss Hudson, why'd you give me an F+?"

"Rashad," she said, kindly, "you quoted *yourself.*"

I didn't see the problem. In fact, it seemed to me that being resourceful should have been worth at least a C+ or a B-.

I challenged, "Is what I wrote true?"

"Yes," she admitted, reluctantly.

"And," I continued, "is what I wrote relevant to the assignment?"

"Yes," she said again, growing impatient with my logic.

"Then why'd I get an F+?" I demanded.

"Rashad, you can't quote yourself," she explained gently.

"Why not?"

"You're not a credible source, sweetie."

I continued to press, "But Miss Hudson, the truth doesn't change, right?"

Her face told me that her mind wasn't changing, either. Miss Hudson explained that research papers needed credible sources, beyond the author, who could be trusted.

"So you're telling me that I've got to go out and do something amazing, or go to school for twenty years, before I can be a credible enough source to come back and say the exact same things?"

"Well," she reasoned, "*yes.*"

Since going to school for twenty years did not appeal, I decided that the way for me to become the "source" whose opinions mattered was to excel in some other way. I wasn't sure what that way would be just yet, but I was determined to show Miss Hudson I could do it. (Stay tuned—we'll come back to this story later in the book!)

Despite my creativity—or perhaps because of it—English wasn't the only class in which I faced—and caused—challenges.

In history class, Mr. Sanderson asked us to write a paper about why Robert E. Lee was a great general. Lee had served as the top army commander of the Confederate States of America. And as far as I could tell, no one in the class questioned his legendary status as an American leader.

Except me.

But not for reasons you might expect.

Mr. Sanderson wheeled out the TV and VCR cart to show us a video that featured a reenactment of a battle from the Civil War. I watched two opposing armies with hundreds of soldiers lined up facing each other with an open area between them. To me, it looked like they were about to do a Soul Train line. Then, at the sound of their commander's voice, they charged one another, ensuring certain death for many of the soldiers on the front line. The whole time, the actor playing General Lee was standing back and watching his men get slaughtered.

This, I thought to myself, *is the dumbest thing I've ever seen!*

When the video ended, there were still fifteen minutes left before the end of class, for questions. My hand shot up in the air. I had a *lot* of questions about the worst strategy I'd ever seen.

"Yes, Rashad." Poor Mr. Sanderson had no idea what was coming.

"For starters, why is everyone lined up and ready to get killed? Why doesn't the general have soldiers staking out the other side, or tripping people, or setting traps or something?"

Mr. Sanderson sighed. "Does anyone have a *serious* question or comment?" he asked, scanning the room for willing students.

He totally dismissed my question, but I was serious. I'd watched my brothers as they led their football teams, as they led their families, as they led in their churches, and as they led me. And they were the kind of leaders who'd take a bullet for the people they were leading. This Lee guy could have taken a lesson from Butch and Bryan. To me as a kid, he wasn't a strategist, and he didn't seem to care very much about his men if he was willing to let them die without fighting alongside them.

"Mr. Sanderson, I am serious," I continued. "Why is Lee considered a good leader when he's got his men lined up to be killed while he's in the back, all safe and protected?"

"Rashad," Mr. Sanderson replied, "you're disrupting class."

Unsatisfied, I conceded, "All right, all right . . ."

Though I was finished for that day, I continued to ask a lot of questions. God had given me both a curious mind and a determined spirit. Asking questions was one of those significant *ifs* in my life. Yes, if I hadn't asked all the questions I did, I might have stayed on teachers' good sides! But I also wouldn't have learned as much as I did. Whenever an adult asked me to believe what they were telling me, the next word out of my mouth would be "Why?" I have always wanted to know why things are the way they are, and that youthful passion for understanding I had is one that still moves me today.

◆ ◆ ◆

When people get exasperated with your questions, it can feel like the easiest thing to do is to stop asking. So in order to avoid making waves, that's what some of us do. We accept whatever we're told because it's easier. But I want to encourage you to notice that resistance you get when you ask *why,* and press through it! That doesn't mean you should be a pain or annoying, but having an inquisitive mind is a really good thing, even if it's not always convenient for others! If you want to keep learning and growing, I encourage you to be bold and brave with your questions.

Setting the Record Straight

Although I gave in to Mr. Sanderson in history class, there were other days that I didn't back down. I asked questions, challenged teachers, and spoke my mind. As a result, I spent a good bit of time in in-school suspension. It didn't bother me that much because I liked the opportunity to get my work done and then chill. In some ways, suspension was better than sitting in class and listening to lectures I was not allowed to participate in.

But I didn't feel so great when I got handed an out-of-school suspension for interrupting a teacher with too many questions. Kids would start laughing whenever my hand went up. I may have been the only student labeled a class clown who was actually serious about his reasons for disrupting class.

Whenever I was suspended, Mom had to take a sick day from her job to stay home with me, and she wasn't happy about it. I tried to persuade her that the teachers were picking on me. I asked legitimate questions and they treated me like I was a troublemaker. Although Mom usually took my side, when it came to school she was more willing to believe the teachers. I knew better than to talk back to my mother, but I was irked that she'd choose to take their word over mine. Still, I couldn't help but start thinking that maybe I was the one in the wrong. Was it bad to ask questions, to challenge authority? Was I being disrespectful and not even realizing it?

One day, after Mom and I had eaten lunch, our home phone rang. I was close enough to hear the voice on the other end.

"Is Mrs. Jennings home?" the voice asked.

"This is Mrs. Jennings," Mom confirmed.

"This is Miss Dixon, calling from the main office at Jefferson Forest High."

I leaned in even closer because now I was really curious. Miss Dixon was the secretary I had to talk to whenever teachers sent me to the office with a referral slip for bad behavior.

"Mrs. Jennings," Miss Dixon reported, "your son was disruptive in class today. Mrs. Overby sent a referral down here to the office."

At last, I had proof of the teachers' conspiracy against me!

"SEE?!?!" I sprung from my chair and hollered at Mom. "I TOLD YOU!"

Some other kid had been goofing off in class, and I was being blamed for it! Now my mom could see what I had to deal with every day. She proceeded to let Miss Dixon know that I had not been at school that day, and asked for her to pass that on to Mrs. Overby as well.

"Do you believe me now?" I asked the moment she hung up the phone.

"Yes, Shaddy Rock," she softly said, flashing her sweet smile and giving me a hug. "I believe you."

I loved it when she used her special pet name for me. I don't even remember when she started calling me that, but it always reminded me that I was *hers*. Grateful for Mom's renewed confidence, I decided I was going to get to the bottom of the issues at school.

When I returned to school after my suspension, I'd had enough. Tired of teachers treating me like I was a problem child, I decided to handle my business myself and my way.

I wanted to call a meeting with all my teachers and the principal, but since no one took me very seriously, I didn't believe they'd show up if I invited them myself. So I penned a handwritten note for all seven of my teachers in what I believed to be the sloppy handwriting style of Principal Francis. It read, "We need to have a meeting about Rashad. Please meet me in the teacher's lounge during lunch tomorrow." One by one, I dropped a note on each teacher's desk, with a gloomy look on my face as if the principal had forced me to deliver them. Not at all confident I could imitate the beautiful penmanship most of my teachers used, I enlisted seven different girls I knew to forge letters to the principal saying, "Hey, we need to have a meeting with you tomorrow about Rashad. Lunchtime in the teacher's lounge."

Thursday at lunchtime I grabbed a cafeteria tray, went through the lunch line to get my chicken nuggets, tater tots, chocolate milk, and Mickey Mouse ice cream, and then marched upstairs to see if my plan had worked.

I was delighted to find that everyone who was invited was actually able to attend. Setting my tray down on a table, I announced, "I called this meeting."

The principal, who'd received letters from seven different teachers all proposing a Thursday lunchtime meeting to discuss me, frowned. "I thought something was weird."

I didn't give them a chance to leave the meeting before I got my concerns out. "I don't know why I'm in trouble all the time," I said. "Am I really that bad?"

They all laughed.

"See! That's exactly what happens! I have something serious to ask or say, and you all laugh like you did just now! I'm tired of everybody saying stuff about me. If you've got something constructive to say to me, then say it now!"

I scanned the faces of those in attendance, to see if anyone would speak up. For better or for worse, no one did. And I'm happy to report that I didn't find myself in trouble with teachers after that gathering.

The One Who Answers

I have always wanted to know *why* things are the way they are, and I rarely swallowed any old answer an adult offered me. (As you might expect, not all the adults in my life appreciated this about me.)

But when I read the Bible, I noticed that throughout Scripture people were asking questions of God. Cain wanted to know *if* he was responsible for his brother's whereabouts. The writers of the Psalms wanted to know *if* God would deliver them. In case the Israelites asked Moses God's name, Moses asked *if* God would reveal his holy name to him. And Jesus asked plenty of questions of those who were for him and those who were against him. I knew that God was someone who welcomed my questions.

What was more curious, I thought, was that God asked lots of questions! He asked Adam, "Where are you?" (Genesis 3:9). God asked Jacob, "What is your name?" (Genesis 32:27).

He asked Satan, "Where have you come from?" (Job 1:7). Why, I wondered, did a God who knew everything need to ask questions?

I won't say that God spoke to me in an audible voice, but I did hear the Spirit's whisper with the ears of my heart, "I ask questions to *teach*." God doesn't ask questions because he doesn't know the answers. When God asks questions, it's so *we* can learn something.

I don't think I understood that fully when I was in high school. But as God grew me and began to teach me more about myself, I understood that wanting to get answers and being inquisitive wasn't the bad thing some of my teachers had made me feel it was. God gave me a mind that wanted to know "why," and that was actually a *good* thing!

Maybe there are things in your life that you have questions about. You may not be concerned with the leadership style of General Robert E. Lee, but you might have questions about things that are more personal. Maybe you want to know why you've faced challenges that not every person has to face. Maybe you want to know why your parents' marriage ended. Maybe you want to know why people can be so cold and cruel sometimes. God welcomes your questions.

God hears your voice and listens when you speak. So ask your hard questions! God can take it. Offer the concerns of your heart to God. Trust me, God's not the teacher who wants to shut you up or send you to the office with a referral slip. God loves to hear from you, and God answers. Sometimes that answer comes through Scripture. Sometimes the messenger might be another person, like a pastor, parent, or mentor. Other times, you might discern God's will through prayer.

God welcomes your big questions. Keep asking them.

CHAPTER 4

YOU DON'T DEFINE ME

I'd been labeled as "disruptive" and a "troublemaker" by my teachers, but I knew those labels didn't capture who I really was. I wasn't willing to let teachers or anyone else for that matter, decide who I was.

A school friend of mine named Janie Henderson invited me to her house a few times, but I was always busy and unable to accept her offer. One day, though, when she invited me over after school to join her family for dinner, I was finally able to accept.

Janie, her brother and sister, and I cranked some country music in the car and had a fun ride to her house, where Janie introduced me to her mother.

"Hi, Rashad," Janie's mom said, folding me in a big hug. "It's so nice to finally meet you! Janie's told me so much about you."

We chatted with Janie's mom in the kitchen for a while, munching on the Rice Krispie treats she'd made for us. She was really nice, and her warmth reminded me of my own mom. Then Janie and her brother and I hung out in the basement and goofed off, watching *The Fresh Prince of Bel Air.* Although I'd never been to Janie's neighborhood before, their home—the home of a white family in a white neighborhood—didn't feel that different from my own.

Around six o'clock her mother called downstairs, "Dad's home! Time for dinner!"

We flipped off the TV and climbed the stairs to get ready for dinner.

When we got upstairs, Janie's dad was looking at the mail. Glancing my way, he dropped his eyes back toward the letters and catalogs.

"Hey, sir," I said, with a big smile. "How are you doing?"

Mr. Henderson didn't respond.

"I'm Rashad," I offered, extending my hand. "It's nice to meet you."

No eye contact. No answer.

Maybe he'd had a bad day.

Not exactly sure what that was about, I joined the others in the dining room. Mrs. Henderson, who I noticed had changed into nicer clothes for dinner, had set six places at the dining room table. And the table looked like it was ready for Thanksgiving! Each porcelain white table setting was framed with silverware and a cloth napkin.

The mood suddenly felt heavier than it had when we first arrived home from school. After Mr. Henderson said a prayer for our meal, we began eating the pot roast, carrots, salad, and potatoes in front of us. I was careful to use my best manners and to not inhale my food the way I usually did. The only sounds in the room were the sounds of silverware.

Thinking that the dinnertime silence was a little odd, I reasoned that maybe everyone was just hungry.

Speaking in the direction of Janie's dad and brother, I asked, "Been watching any games?"

I didn't know anyone who could resist talking football. Yeah, it usually turned into trash talking the other person's team, but it was still fun. Janie's brother mentioned a game they watched a few weeks back, but no one else chimed in.

Feeling the strain of the awkward silence, I exclaimed, "These mashed potatoes are good, Mrs. Henderson!"

After she thanked me, the room fell silent again.

Something was off in that room, but I didn't know what it was. Was it me? Did I have something stuck in my teeth? Did I have a huge booger on my face? Wanting to rule out these possibilities, I politely excused myself to use the restroom.

Walking through the kitchen, I stepped into the bathroom and checked my appearance in the mirror. Clean teeth. No booger.

Then I saw it.

Resting on top of the tank on the back of the toilet were three decorative letters, like you might get at a craft or hobby store. They were displayed the way a college girl might feature her sorority letters. But this wasn't a decorative celebration of Delta Sigma Theta or Zeta Phi Beta.

Three wood block letters read: K.K.K.

Though I'd never encountered anything like it, I knew

that the Klan was a hate group that had opposed the Civil Rights Movement and advocated white supremacy and white nationalism.

My head was spinning. As I mentally replayed the interactions I'd had in Janie's home, they suddenly made more sense: her father not acknowledging me when I introduced myself, the cool mood in the dining room, the silence at the dinner table. I no longer felt safe or comfortable in Janie's home. My mind raced with questions. *How could a home that had felt so much like my own be hiding such an ugly secret? And why on earth would they reveal it by putting it on display? Why hadn't Janie, or her mom, or siblings warned me?* Although I knew my father had faced racism in the military, I'd never encountered anything like this before.

What am I gonna do?

My heart thumped in my chest as I considered my options.

Staying and playing along with the charade didn't feel right. I wanted to get out of there.

I could have grabbed my backpack and run straight through the garage and out into Janie's neighborhood. But that didn't feel quite right, either. Janie's mom and siblings had been really kind, and I didn't want to be rude to them.

I finally settled on returning to the table and announcing my departure. Whispering a prayer to God for help, I opened the bathroom door and returned to the table. I didn't want anyone at the table to see how scared I was. If they had spoken to each other while I was in the restroom, everyone fell silent at my return.

Rather than leaving immediately, I sat back down and tried once more to get a conversation going. After realizing I was getting nowhere, I simply announced, "Look, guys, I'm sorry. I see how it is, and I don't want to disrespect y'all's home. I think I'm going to go now."

Janie yelped, "What? You can't go, Rashad! Please stay! Just finish dinner." While Janie's dad kept his eyes down, I recognized anguish in the rest of the faces at that dinner table.

Undeterred, I announced, "I see where I'm at, and I'm going to excuse myself."

I honestly don't know how I held it together. It was like I was on autopilot and instead of rage, what had bubbled up were all the manners my mom had taught me since I was a young boy.

"No, you don't have to go," Janie's mom said politely.

"Thank you for dinner, Mrs. Henderson," I said. Then I headed for the kitchen, grabbed my backpack, and swiftly stepped out the door.

It had never felt so good to be outside! I had to get some distance from Janie's house to clear my head, so I walked about two blocks before pausing to dig my flip phone out of my backpack to call Mom.

When she picked me up at the entrance to Janie's neighborhood, I didn't mention the reason I'd left so abruptly. I just thanked her for coming to get me and told her I wanted to get home to do my homework.

Compared to sitting at that table, homework was actually appealing.

Back at School

When I was waiting at the bus stop the next morning, chatting with guys I knew my whole life—most of them white—I pushed away thoughts about what had happened the night before. But when we all piled off the bus and headed into school, I noticed that I was more aware of the environment I always took for granted.

The student body at Jefferson Forest—a high school in a rural community outside of Lynchburg—was about ninety percent white and ten percent black, with maybe a couple Latino kids. This was my world, and it seemed completely normal to me. Back then, when the world wasn't as politically charged as it is today, I'd ride around with my football buddies in trucks that had Confederate flags on them. To us, it just made no difference. Not only had my boys and I grown up in the same neighborhoods and attended the same schools, but we'd also worked together on the football field. As fellow team members, what brought us together was bigger than what divided us. From peewee all the way up to the NFL, football has its own set of rules, on and off the field. My friends and I shared a common goal, and that united us.

But as I scanned the parking lot, I began to wonder how many other households were like Janie's. Who else's parents believe what her dad believed? Worse yet, were there students at my school who felt the same way? The protective bubble around my childhood was abruptly popped.

When I spotted Janie's car in the parking lot, I headed in her direction.

I was a little ticked off that she had put me in that position. And although her words and actions proved that she didn't think the way her dad did, I still felt like she had thrown me under the bus. An angry scowl spread over her face, but it wasn't for me.

"I hate that my dad is like that," she said, sounding sad and frustrated. "But if anyone could change his mind, it would be you."

"And how'd that work out for ya?" I asked wryly.

She hung her head. "Rashad," she whispered. "I'm so sorry."

"I forgive you," I said. "But to be clear, I ain't ever going back to your house!"

I was happy to put that night behind me, where it stayed until Janie's father and I would meet again, a few years later.

You Define You

I refused to let that night or anyone define me. And that's how I've always been. When peewee coaches suggested I play the positions that bulky kids played, I ignored them. When my dad predicted that I'd end up like him, I vowed to become someone different. When teachers treated me like I was a clown, I decided to be someone who would be taken seriously. Even as a kid, I had this ever-increasing sense that I mattered to God, and that God had called me worthy. To me, that was all that mattered.

Although they may not be as brazen as Janie's dad, there will always be people who will try to define you and keep you in a box. Older siblings might make you feel puny and worthless. Teachers might not view you as someone who's destined for success. Other adults may lack the vision to see the inherent value you bear as a child of God. Or they'll fail to recognize the amazing potential that's inside of you. And, like me, you may even have a parent, present or absent, who communicates to you that you are insignificant.

You might also find yourself on the receiving end of prejudice. Someone may judge you for things you can't control, like your skin color or the neighborhood where you grew up. Someone may judge you for things important to the core of your identity, like your beliefs or values. These kinds of judgments are the hardest to overcome, and there's no quick fix for dealing with the hurt and frustration that come with prejudice. You just have to keep reminding yourself that those opinions don't matter. They don't change who you are.

I want you to hear loud and clear that no one, except you and God, gets to define you. You have God-given dignity and worth, simply because you exist. And as you decide to live that truth, you also get to decide who you will be. You can choose to ignore the opinions of others as you strive to become the man or woman God created you to be.

No one else gets to define you.

CHAPTER 5

GIVING ONE HUNDRED

The question lingering in my mind as tenth grade drew to close, wasn't whether I wanted to play football the following season. I knew I did. The question was whether or not I'd make the team. When I showed up for summer conditioning, before my junior year, it was painfully—and I do mean *painfully*—obvious that I'd not spent the year getting back into shape. I was wheezing every time I ran. And I was still carrying extra weight. After the first day, my muscles ached. Thankfully, though, the coaches recognized enough skill and drive to bring me back on and let me practice with the running backs as someone who might actually see playing time. My friends, who appreciated my goofy antics in the locker room and practice field, were glad to have me back. I was glad to be hanging around with my boys again despite the fact I knew it was unlikely I would ever set foot on the field during a game.

Most running backs in high school football are around 195 pounds, and I was a hefty 268. Because I was still jawing about playing running back, the coaches continued to allow me to stay with the running backs, creating a fifth string running back position just for me. I know they did it just to shut me up, but it gave me satisfaction. I practiced with the other backs, and we watched film together to dissect how they'd been playing and how they could improve. I was eager to learn everything I could from their performances.

One Hundred

Although I was aware of my shortcomings, I never let go of my dream of being a pro running back. Besides my size, I knew what raw talent looked like. And I was honest with myself about the fact that I didn't have a big share of it. You know who did have it? My brother, Bryan. I observed the way he moved effortlessly on the field. And it wasn't just football, either! He was magic on the basketball court and on the track, as well. Though Bryan gave each practice, game, and meet his all, he was naturally gifted, and didn't have to work as hard as some guys.

That wasn't me.

I had one move, and that was *hard work*. I've always said that I might not have had as much natural talent as the next guy on the field, but I *would* outwork him. I'll put in the time it takes to improve my skills and become excellent. In practice, that meant I was giving everything I had. Some guys would slack off when the coach was busy elsewhere, and others saved their fiercest fire for the game. But every practice I was giving everything I had to improve. When I returned to the field after taking a year off, I knew that it was now or never, so I came back with more passion than ever. Even so, as a kid in my third year of high school, who'd never seen a minute of playing time, it was hard to see when I was going to blossom into the player I believed I could be. For all I knew, it might never happen, no matter how hard I tried.

When I was eight, Butch took me to see the movie *Rudy*. It was about a kid who dreamed of playing for Notre Dame but, for a lot of reasons, was a total underdog. Sound familiar? Rudy even had a learning disability, like me. His challenge was dyslexia and mine was a reading comprehension deficit. When Rudy was finally allowed to transfer to Notre Dame and practice with the team as a walk-on, he won the hearts of the guys on the team. In some ways, I felt like Rudy. All the guys on the team liked me, but the odds of me ever getting playing time in a game were pretty slim.

But every day in practice, I gave 100 percent. At the far end of the field, opposite the scoreboard, was a very steep hill we called the Green Monster. Our coach had us run that hill to build our endurance. Trust me—that hill lived up to its nickname. On wet days we couldn't even attempt it because it was pretty much a vertical surface and so was almost impossible to scale. But when we were sent out to run, I'd give it all I had. At the top of the hill, I'd pull my inhaler out of my pocket and take a deep breath of medicine. Yeah, I felt a little goofy about it, but I did what I had to do. Then I'd shuffle-slide back down, turn around, and climb it again.

That was my junior year. The guy who worked hard even though it didn't immediately pay off. The guy who ran to the top of the Green Monster as fast as he could, but had to stop for a puff of an inhaler at the top. I wasn't the fittest or fastest player on the team—I didn't even know how to get there. But I kept trying, day after day after day. I just kept climbing that Green Monster, hoping that one day, all the pain, sweat, and effort would be worth it.

Opening Game

Our first game of the official season was against Amherst. It was clear to me from my not-so-great workouts and practices that I wasn't going to be seeing playing time, but it was still fun to be a part of the action. I'd missed being on the team last year, hanging out with my friends, trash-talking our opponents, gearing up to go out on the field and play the game.

As we stepped out of the locker room to run through a tunnel of cheerleaders and marching-band members, I felt the excitement of the crowd and the thumping pulse of the band's drums. Football was a big deal in rural Virginia, and our whole town came out to cheer on the Jefferson Forest High School Cavaliers.

As I took my place on the bench, I settled in to watch the game from the best seat in the house. My favorite guy to watch, and also one of the fans' favorites, was my best friend, Maurice, who was a captain on the team. We met when I was seven, when Bryan was dating a great girl named Pam. Whenever Pam would come over and the two of them would snuggle up on the couch, I would wedge myself right in between them. I thought Pam was *my* girlfriend! "Mom!" Bryan would holler through the house. "Get Rashad out of here!" I was really annoying. But my Pam was a smart cookie, and so she started bringing over her little brother, Maurice, who was my age, to distract me. And it worked! Maurice and I became best friends. And by the time we were in high school, Bryan and Pam had married.

In that first game against Amherst, which we won, Maurice played an amazing game. If he wasn't my best friend, I might have been jealous of him because, in a lot of ways, he was living the life I'd always imagined for myself. As a six-year-old kid, I wouldn't have even conceived of the possibility that I'd still be warming the bench a decade later. But Maurice was my boy. He was a really talented quarterback and safety, and I loved cheering him on. It would have been more fun to be in the huddle with him, but, as I'd expected, I spent that whole game on the bench. I didn't mind too much, because Monday was coming.

Scout

For me, Monday afternoon was my version of Friday night under the lights. Our first-string defense needed someone to practice against, and so the coaches had scrubs like me, guys who weren't ready to be starters, play on the scout team. As the scout team running back, I approached every day of practice as if everything depended on it. Practice was the only game day I had. So I did all the things first-string players did on game days. I wrapped my wrists. I used eye black. I put spat on my shoes, taping them for extra ankle support. I took everything about these scrimmages seriously. Only the coaches watched these games, but they were my audience.

When the scout team did well, the coaches would be furious, and they'd lay into the first-string guys.

"If you can't beat these scrubs, how are you going to beat the other team's starters on Friday night?"

This always pleased me. It wasn't about beating my teammates—it was about proving to myself that I could win, even though I never got to play for real.

At that point, I wasn't nearly as good as the starters, but I played like I was one of those fierce little yappy dogs who has no idea he's small and weak. I didn't back down or back off, even when I should have. But *that*—giving everything I had, in practice—was my way of getting better. It was my preparation for that one magical future day when Coach would send me in to play for our team. I prayed and prayed that day would come, but as the season wore on, it seemed less likely it would come to pass.

I spent the first four days of the week giving 110 percent in practice. Then when game day rolled around, I'd suit up in my uniform and I'd hide candy where my thigh pads should have been, for easier snack access during the game. I didn't even bother tying my cleats. I just prepared to take it easy on the bench. During these games, one thought would fill my mind: *I can't wait until Monday.* On Monday, I'd get to play again. On Monday, I'd have the chance to prove myself again. On Monday, I'd get to do the thing I loved. On Monday, I'd get to *work hard*.

Trailing behind the starters as we dashed through the human tunnel, my friend Speedy and I ran out onto the field with the team and then bee-lined straight to our spots on the bench.

"Hey, man," Speedy asked me. "You got the Sprites?"

He knew I did. I always wrapped up a few cans of Sprite with white medical tape so that it wouldn't be as obvious that we were kicking back, drinking soda, and sneaking M&Ms during the game. As far as we were concerned, Speedy and I had front row seats at the best show in town.

I accepted my role as spectator and number one fan during the games because I knew I always had Monday.

When we don't yet see the results we want to see, it can be tempting to slack off. It can be hard to find a reason to keep investing in our dreams when we don't see the fruits of our work. I know what it feels like when the dream seems out of reach. Believe me, every outward sign—asthma, my weight, my lack of playing time—seemed to suggest that I would have been a better water boy, or team mascot, than running back. But I still wasn't willing to give up.

That season, practicing with the scout team was a valuable time of preparation for me. It meant that whether we were conditioning or scrimmaging, I was going all out.

For a musician, it might mean practicing for hours on end when no one else is listening. For actors, it may mean allowing a script to live in your heart as you prepare to give life to a character. For runners, it means logging mile after mile before you ever set foot on a racecourse. When you give one-hundred percent effort, you're preparing for the success you see in your mind.

I'll admit that it took a pretty creative imagination to visualize success, given the realities of being a junior who was a fifth-string running back and didn't play. But despite the odds, and without a clear path to success, I still hadn't given up on the dream that had been growing in my heart for as long as I could remember.

The frustrated little kid who'd been stuck as an offensive lineman in peewee league had morphed into someone who could finally embrace his role as a scrub. That doesn't mean that I'd given up or even that I'd accepted my role as fifth-string running back. I hadn't and I didn't. But I'd finally learned to find the silver linings in situations I wouldn't have chosen for myself.

I know you've been in situations like that too. Maybe it's in an athletic competition, a school club, or leadership role, or even an afterschool job. Every time you find yourself in a position you didn't choose, or completing a task you'd rather not be doing, you can choose to make the most of that opportunity. You can use it to grow.

And who knows who or what you'll grow into . . . maybe the very person you've dreamed of being.

CHAPTER 6

THE BIG GAME

Neither Speedy nor I saw even one minute of playing time during the first nine conference games of our junior year at Jefferson Forest High School. Though I was eager to improve, and to prove myself to my coaches, we were happy enough to snack on the sidelines and talk smack about what we'd do if we were out on the field. Every game, we were in our own little world.

The Cavaliers' last game of the season was against our crosstown rivals, the Brookville Bees. When I say crosstown rivals, I don't mean these were guys from the other side of the county who we didn't know. I mean there was an arbitrary line drawn between the two school zones, right between a couple homes in a residential neighborhood, dividing long-time neighbors and friends. This was even the place where we met to settle differences with fist fights. For years, the Bees and the Cavaliers had been archenemies. The teams' rivalry off the field ranged from playing pranks—like spray painting obscene pictures on the other teams' playing field—to fist fights in parking lots. Every time we played Brookville, the game sold out. The schools even had to hire extra security to keep fans and players safe.

Brookville was the last game of my junior year. Because our record was five and four, we already knew we wouldn't be advancing to the playoffs. But, because Brookville had won a few more games than we had, they'd advance if they beat us in that final game. Either way, it was our last game, but we had fire in our bellies to keep Brookville from advancing. If we weren't moving ahead, then neither were they.

The Friday night game was held at Jefferson Forest. The bleachers were packed, and people were sitting on blankets, lining the grassy hills on either side of the stands. Little kids tossed nerf footballs with their friends, like I used to at Bryan's games. The smell of warm, buttery popcorn wafted through the crowd as our team ran out onto the field to the roaring madness of the crazy Cavalier fans. As the quarter-back broke through the tape and led us to the sidelines, we were all amped up, ready to defeat the Brookville Bees.

As I jogged onto the field, I heard someone shouting my name, "Rashad! Rashad Jennings, let's go! You got this!"

It was the first time I'd ever heard my name being called on a football field! Turning toward the sound, I saw Butch and Bryan pressed against the outside fence, grinning and encouraging me. It was the first game they'd attended together that year because of their coaching schedule conflict. They were both high school football coaches at a local private school in Lynchburg, Virginia, and even though we all knew I'd be riding the pine, my heart swelled at their support.

When Speedy and I reached the benches, we fist bumped, took off our helmets, tossed them aside, and settled in with our snacks for what promised to be an amazing game. We heard that several college scouts were there to look at some of our players, including a scout from Tennessee who came to see our starting running back, Quincy Freeman.

Speedy and I watched as our captains shook hands with the Bees' captains and the ref tossed the coin. When the ref announced that we'd be receiving first, the crowd stomped the bleachers, creating a deep rumble as the background to their screams and shouts.

Stepping to the line of scrimmage, our quarterback, Doug Jones, put his hands under center and barked, "Blue 80, Blue 80, Hut-Hut!" The center snapped the ball.

Quincy took the handoff and picked up about five yards before he was tackled. After the whistle, players began to clear away, but Quincy didn't get up. He sat up in the grass, but didn't stand. When the ref gave our coach a nod and a wave, players from both teams took a knee as both Coach Smith and our head athletic trainer jogged out onto the field to check on Quincy. When the trainer knelt beside him, asking him to move his foot, I saw Quincy's face clench in agony. After a few more minutes of testing, the trainer and Coach helped Quincy to his feet, and fans of both teams stood together and showed their support by clapping with respect.

When I saw Quincy limping, favoring his left foot and pro-tecting his right, I figured he'd rolled his ankle.

I knew what an injury—major or minor—meant for Quincy and our team. This game was supposed to be his moment to wow the scouts, and that once-in-a-lifetime opportunity had gone out the window with one twist of an ankle. Our chance of winning the game might have gone out the window too. It was going to be a lot harder to beat Brookville without him.

I took a quick swig of Sprite.

Speedy turned to me and asked, with the excitement of a kid at Christmas, "Aw, man! Shad, you think you're gonna play?"

I shook my head. "Come on, man! You know they ain't gonna play me. I'm fifth-string," I reminded him. I had no expectation my bench warming would change that night.

Speedy and I both knew that the back-up running back was going to step in for Quincy. He'd do a great job and the whole team would rally. I poured some M&Ms into Speedy's open hand.

As play resumed, Jay Spinner, our second string running back, jogged onto the field and joined the huddle. The first play, Doug got sacked. The second play, Doug handed off to Jay and he sprinted about four yards before he stumbled and went down. Doug gave Jay a hand, but when he stood up, he wasn't able to put weight on his left leg. He looked to the side-lines to catch Coach's eye, and pointed to his hamstring. Two down. As Jay hopped off the field, Coach sent in our third string back, Tim Hunter.

At that moment, I felt like I was being watched, and

sure enough, as I glanced at Speedy, I caught him, eyes wide open as if he saw a ghost. Mouth opened, filled with half-eaten M&Ms, he blurted out the same question he'd asked me minutes before.

"Hey! Rashad, you think they're gonna play you?"

"Nah," I assured him. "There ain't no way in the world."

It was clear that both teams were out for blood, so it probably wouldn't be the last injury of the game. But I knew that the odds of four players playing the same position being injured in the same game were unlikely.

Yet I had to admit I was starting to feel a little nervous when Coach sent in the third-string running back. Tim Hunter was in the P.E. class right after mine, and earlier that week, on the volleyball court, I saw him acting up. He was showing off for girls, doing back handsprings. Some of us warned him, "Take it easy, you're going to hurt yourself." But he didn't listen. When Tim hurt his wrist earlier in the week, we told him what a fool he was. The damage was done, and to top it off, he wasn't being smart about it. He actually kept his injury hidden from the coaches and the trainer, and of course, no one ratted on him.

Because Doug knew Tim's left wrist was messed up, he put the ball right in Tim's gut, so Tim could wrap his left arm around the ball. Tim dipped past the first defender, but then got hit. Coach, who could tell something wasn't right, called Tim over to the side, and pulled him out. It was a shame, because he could *run*. Coach sent in Jake Rogers, the Cavaliers' fourth-string running back.

That's when I started to get *really* nervous.

Eyes even wider, Speedy started in again. "Hey, Rashad, they down again—"

The butterflies in my stomach began to build as the reality that I could actually get in the game started to set in.

Even if you're not a football player, you can recognize the absurdity of three people who play the same position being injured in the same game. And now Jake was in. If Jake was injured and unable to play—which, with the string of bad luck we'd faced was suddenly feeling very possible—there wasn't anyone left *but* me. No longer interested in Sprite and M&Ms, I felt my heart racing.

Lord, I prayed, *protect Jake out there on the field.*

Jake was in the game for about four plays when he was tackled at a weird angle and blew out his knee at the thirty-yard line. When the ref signaled our coach to come out on the field, the crowds that had been roaring all evening fell eerily silent. Knowing Jake had never even made it out onto the field before, Cavalier fans had no idea what would happen next. Neither did I.

Peering along the sideline, Coach started scanning those of us still on the bench. Terror and excitement pulsed through my body.

Speedy, now hyped beyond belief, was shaking me by the shoulders. I glanced over at the coach who was still surveying his prospects, searching for anyone other than me.

This is it! It's gonna be me! There's no one left! I'm the only other guy who plays running back!

Looking right past me, Coach sent in Jimmy Talbert, our backup receiver. Part of me wanted to be outraged at not being considered, but the rest of me was relieved because I was so nervous. I started cheering for Jimmy louder than anyone.

I wish I could say that Jimmy held his own out there, but he did terribly. He kept messing up, running the wrong play. I glanced at Coach out of the corner of my eye and I could see that he was furious.

"Get him out!" he yelled to no one in particular, but loud enough for half the stadium to hear him.

He called a timeout and ordered Jimmy, "You're out."

Looking around again in utter frustration, realizing he had no other option, he hollered, "Where's Jennings?"

As I sat dazed, Speedy started poking me and shaking me violently. "Yes! Shad! He called you!"

Although I'd imagined this moment for years—being just the man the team needed in a pinch—I'd always imagined my coach being happier about putting me in.

Waving his clipboard toward the field, Coach yelled, "Jennings, get in the game!"

I snapped out of my reverie, scrambling to find my helmet.

Although I'd had it on my head when the team ran through the tunnel and onto the field, it never once occurred to me that I'd need to *wear* it in the game. The odds seemed like a million to one. I grabbed the nearest helmet and as I was putting it on my head, I realized it was way too big.

I'm sure I looked like a bobble-head doll, but I didn't care. Noticing the mouthpiece dangling from the face mask, I thought, "That is too nasty. There is no way I'm putting that in my mouth." So I ripped it off and dropped it on the ground.

As I ran out to join the guys who were already huddling up on the field, it felt like one of those dreams where you show up to school naked. I felt the eyes of hundreds of fans as I jogged onto the field to join the players I always battled as a member of the scout team. For the first time, we were on the same side. As I tried to pay attention to the quarterback's instructions, my mind was racing.

Will I make a complete fool of myself?

Will I do better than Jimmy Talbert?

Every practice for the previous eleven years had brought me to this moment of truth. I could hear Speedy and my other friends on the bench going crazy, but I also knew the guys on the field were thinking, "What are you doing here!?"

Not Maurice, though. He had a big grin on his face and slapped my butt as I joined the huddle. And another captain, our tight end, John Hamlet, was also one of my boys.

"Shad's in," John announced, declaring my legitimacy the way a king would dub a knight. "Let's go!"

John had already been recruited by UNC, and when I played scout defense, I played defensive end against him. One day after practice he'd remarked, "Rashad, you're good." I still treasured those words and his confidence in me.

As I scanned the faces of the other players, I could read that no one was *mad* that I was on the field. They all liked me. I imagined each one was probably thinking, "Shad's my boy, but I don't know what he's gonna do out there." To be fair, neither did I.

Doug Jones, our quarterback, said, "We're gonna do 44 dive. Got it? On three: one, two, three, Cavaliers!"

I knew that play inside and out. I spent a lot of time rehearsing this scene over and over in practice. It was etched in my mind and even in my muscle memory. But the rest of me was freaking out. This was the biggest moment of my life so far and I wanted to make it count.

As the huddle broke up, I confirmed, "Doug, the run is to the right, right?"

I knew that it was, but I felt so shaky.

"Yeah," he confirmed, "it's *right.*"

I was so nervous I could hardly think straight. I'd spent hundreds of hours on that field, but not at night with the lights on, and certainly not under the watchful gaze of hundreds of Cavaliers fans whose hearts were set on victory.

We all assumed our places and got into position. I was the furthest back on the field and could see everything.

Bending his knees, Doug looked left, looked right, and then growled, "Blue eighty!"

In the middle of the count, I freaked out and yelled, "Hey, Doug!"

I don't know what I was expecting Doug to say or do. I just panicked.

Doug continued, "Blue eighty! Set . . . hut."

It was show time.

Game On

Although I knew what it said, I instinctively glanced up at the scoreboard. It was the bottom of the first quarter, and the game was tied at 0–0. As I went through the steps of the play that had been burned into my mind, I felt like I was moving in slow motion. Doug extended his left arm with the ball, but I was a step slow getting there. Still, I was able to grab the ball at the forty-yard line with a lineman bearing down on me. I sidestepped him and found a seam in the defense's line. I picked up speed with that big ol' helmet bobbling around on my head. A few defenders tried to bring me down, but I was on my way. Feeling like I was in a dream, I pumped my legs as fast as they would carry me. After about fifteen yards, I had left the defense in the dust.

The crowd was going berserk. The band was banging on their drums and the metal bleachers were quaking as fans stomped and pounded. Dads were hollering. Cheerleaders were screaming. It was absolute chaos. And for those last twenty-five yards, I felt like I was flying. My stride opened up, and between each touch of my cleats on the ground—right, left, right, left—I really felt like I was soaring.

When I reached the end zone, I turned my head and saw two Brookville players who were chasing me slow to a jog and stop. I gulped in deep breaths of air.

As this turn of events was so wildly unexpected, I was completely unprepared with a signature end zone dance. The boy in me wanted to do the dirty bird, but if I'd flapped my wings I would have looked more like a Brookville Bee than a Jefferson Forest Cavalier. Freaking out, exploding with energy, I threw the football into the air. Ideally it would have returned to earth somewhere near the field, but I was so riled up that I chucked it all the way into the woods.

As the ref raised his arms to signal a touchdown, I was still completely out-of-my-mind crazy. With nothing left to throw, I slammed my oversized helmet onto the ground. Unfortunately, the earpiece popped off and hit the ref in the leg.

Wide-eyed, I apologized to the ref, "Hey, ref, you okay, sir? I'm so sorry!"

Stone faced, dropping his arms from the touchdown sign, he grabbed a yellow flag and tossed it for excessive celebration.

Coming on the heels of the best moment of my entire life, it was a consequence I could live with. Not even a flag could bring me down.

I glanced up toward the stands and saw Butch and Bryan jumping around like madmen. My teammates gathered around, chest-bumping me and slapping my bare head. Now that we'd pulled ahead of Brookville by six, we were going bananas. Although I knew Coach had to be pleased, he also wanted us to demonstrate a little bit of dignity.

"Jennings!" he yelled.

I was waiting for him to praise me for my amazing forty-yard run, but he didn't.

Instead, he bellowed, "Act like you been there before!"

With a big, bright smile across my face, I yelled back, "Hey, Coach! I never been there before!"

As I glanced at the guys on the bench, who were *my people*, one of them hollered, "Represent!"

I wasn't just playing for the Cavaliers that night, I was playing for the boys on the bench.

And Speedy?

Speedy lost his mind! He was still hopping around screaming. As I jogged toward the sideline, he tapped his hand on his numbers, signaling that we were about to chest bump. Mind you, at this time I'm 268 pounds, and Speedy was probably 180 soaking wet. When we jumped up in the air to chest bump, Speedy ended up falling to the ground. I laughed, and when I reached down to give him a hand up, he pulled me down with him.

"Want some M&Ms?" he chirped, as he hopped back up.

"Yeah, man," I answered.

Pulling my inhaler from under the bench where I'd stashed it, I took a quick puff. As we were watching our defense, Speedy just kept talking.

"It was great!" he repeated over and over.

And a few minutes later he exclaimed, "Shad, you did it! You really did it!"

That boy was talking to me like I hadn't even been there when I did it. I saw the athletic trainer taping up Quincy's right ankle, and the trainer gave coach the thumbs up that he was ready to go back in the game. I'd had my moment, and I didn't even dare to imagine that it was ever going to get any better than scoring that touchdown.

But then it did.

Taking a Break

I'd found my assigned helmet and was busy "rehydrating" with the Sprite I'd brought for Speedy and me when our team got the ball back and the offense ran back onto the field. Feeling a bit relieved to see Quincy back in the game, and knowing that this was supposed to be his big night to impress the Tennessee scout, I put down the Sprite, clapped my hands together, and cheered him on. Because he was walking gingerly on that ankle, I knew he was still hurting. Every player tells the trainer and the coach, "I'm all right," whether they are or not.

After the first play, when Doug fumbled the ball, it was really obvious that Quincy wasn't going to make it through the game. Favoring his left side, there was no way he was going to be able to perform out there.

When Coach called a timeout, Quincy limped off the field. Even though I had spent three years gunning for the starting spot, I felt really bad for Quincy.

"Jennings!" the coach yelled. "Get in!"

Throwing on my own helmet this time, and sucking in my own mouth guard, I jogged out onto the field.

As Quincy and I passed, he grabbed me by the shoulders and told me, "Go kill it!"

How classy is that? Quincy knew how hard I worked and he was a great friend to encourage me. It couldn't have been easy for him, not when he had so much riding on that game.

When I joined the huddle this time, the other ten guys were pumped to have me there.

"Okay, it's between Jennings and Hunter."

Hunter was the running back who tried to play with an injured wrist. He could run, but he had to carry the ball in his left hand.

Together we did what we were trained to do and, play by play, hit by hit, pass by pass, we marched the ball down the field. We were pass blocking and picking up blitzes.

I heard the coaches on the sidelines yelling, "That's great, Jennings!"

I caught a screen and picked up a first down.

On third and twenty, Doug flicked me the ball. Dodging a linebacker, I made it into the secondary, the defensive backfield, and took off.

One of Brookville's safeties reached me just before I stepped into the end zone, but I dragged him with me and landed over the line, still gripping the ball.

Even though I was a big guy, I popped up like a jack in the box when the crowd started cheering! Once again, I was grinning from ear to ear.

Bursting with energy, I was about to throw the ball, but the ref eyeballed me.

Looking me in the eyes, as if willing me to stay in control, the ref raised his arms to signal my second touchdown.

Unable to wipe the stupid grin off my face, I told him, "Hey, sir, my bad about the earpiece."

He remained expressionless, but my smile got bigger.

The "Why"

I knew that what was happening out on the field was blowing the fans' minds. And on one level, it was blowing my mind as well! But that part of me that had dreamed I'd be a successful running back was experiencing what I always knew was achievable. And the "if" that made it possible had to do with the hustle I continually gave at practice. But what I was experiencing was my first taste of a principle I've grown to cherish and live by: "Always give one-hundred percent, because when the opportunity comes, it's too late to prepare." When the teacher tells you to put your books away and take out a pencil for the test, it's too late to study. When you show up at the DMV to get your driver's license, it's too late to learn your traffic signs. When it's time to fill out college applications, it's too late to start bringing up your GPA. But when you consistently hustle to do your best in every circumstance, you're going to be ready when opportunity comes knocking.

Sprinting to the sidelines, I glanced at Speedy and tapped my numbers. As I went in for the chest bump, Speedy stuck out his arm to shake my hand, instead.

"Man," he exclaimed, "you my hero! How's it feel?!"

It felt pretty good.

CHAPTER 7

MORE SURPRISES

At halftime, Speedy and I headed off toward the locker room together. Guys sat in chairs—offense on the left, defense on the right. Those who played always sat closer to the whiteboard to hear Coach go over what we had done and what we needed to do. As always, I hung with my friends from the bench in the back of the group, by the lockers, as Coach reviewed the game on the overhead projector.

He was breaking down one of the plays we ran when he looked up, scanned the room, and located me.

"Jennings, get to the front."

Pleased, I pressed through the crowd of guys and squatted down in front. I was grinning from ear to ear. I was used to goofing off, so I hit the guy's butt next to me, whispering, "Hey, what's up man?"

I did not know how to handle myself.

"Pay attention!" he whispered.

I forgot I was supposed to be serious, because I felt like a little kid at the amusement park. But if Coach was going to keep me in the game, which I desperately hoped he would, I had to be up to speed. Willing myself to be serious, I focused on the coach's words.

On the way out of the locker room, players were hitting me on the back, encouraging me to keep going.

"Hey, Rashad, we're proud of you."

"Keep doing your thing."

Back in the game at the top of the third quarter, our defensive ends and linebackers kept getting hurt. It was just like what happened to the offense in the first half of the game. One defensive end went down. A second defensive end went down. Coaches moved a linebacker to the line and he got hurt too.

I was watching and thinking, *What in the world?*

I overheard our starting tight end say, "Coach, Jennings is better than half those dudes! I go against him every day. Put Jennings in!"

And before I knew it, I was playing defensive end. So not only was I playing in my first game ever, but now I was playing a position I didn't know. I lined up beside two guys I'd known for years. One was one of the best linebackers I ever played with.

"I like seeing you in!" he said, as he patted me on the butt. "Let's go, Jennings."

When the Brookville's quarterback said "Hike," I came off the edge, pulling a swing move on the offensive tackle who was trying to block me and making him miss. The quarterback was sitting in the pocket, looking for a receiver. He was about to throw the ball when I came from his blind side. I hit him and knocked the mess out of him. The crowd went wild.

Every player, on the Bees and on the Cavaliers, yelled, "Fumble!"

I heard "fumble" as I was driving the quarterback to the ground, and I realized the ball was loose. I shot up, picked up the ball, and ran it in for my third touchdown—this time on *defense*!

"Hey, man," I said to the referee, all ecstatic and super-confident, "get used to seeing me!" I was trying so hard to get that guy to smile, and he wouldn't break.

Moments later, I headed back out onto the field. Having scored all three of our team's touchdowns, I pinched myself to make sure I wasn't dreaming. The score was now 21–24, Brookville, and they had the ball. There was one minute and nineteen seconds left in the game. We needed to find a way to get the football back in our hands.

Coach called a timeout and the players on the field ran in. Looking my way, he said, "Jennings, we need you."

What?! They were words I'd only dreamed of hearing.

So I joined the huddle with Coach on the sideline. As someone who'd found peace with my role as a supporting member of the team, this was the first moment I truly felt like I was an equal to the rest of the guys who'd been playing all year.

Maurice called a cover two blitz, rushing the quarterback to disrupt any attempt to pass. We came off the edge and I got the sack, then we called a timeout right away. Now there was one minute left. Next play: second down and fifteen, and Brookville ran the ball. I knew that all they had to do was run the clock out and punt on fourth down if needed. But the running back only got about three yards before we called another timeout.

We still had fifty seconds on the clock. It was third down and twelve. At defensive end, I was searching for every possible cue from their offense for what was about to happen. I noticed that their running back scanned the field way too much, giving me every indication that they might not be running the ball this time, which would have been the natural play to make. I wondered why he was looking around when all they had to do was run the ball and end the game.

When the Brookville quarterback dropped back, I felt a screen play developing because the Bees' offensive lineman was supposed to block me, but he didn't. Because I put in so many years on the scout team, I knew just what that meant!

This was one of those fortunate "if" moments for me. While a lot of guys I played with saw scout team as "second best," I saw it as the best training ground for becoming the player I wanted to be. Because of the countless hours I put into those scrimmages, I learned to sense what was happening on the field as it was happening. If I had given up because I wasn't seeing playing time, I would not have been prepared for that important moment.

Reading the backfield, I snuck behind the offensive linemen as they were running out. The quarterback, who didn't see me, threw the ball to the running back for a screen. But, anticipating where the ball was going, I intercepted it out of nowhere, catching everyone by surprise. And running it forty yards, I scored again!

The End Is Near

With thirty-four seconds left in the game, we kicked off and Brookville ran one pass play, which was incomplete. They had to end the game with a Hail Mary, which was unsuccessful, and the crowd erupted into a deafening roar when the final whistle blew. Fans wearing Jefferson Forest colors rushed onto the field, almost tearing down a goalpost in their excitement. I even caught a glimpse of Butch and Bryan near the forty-yard line, giving me thumbs up and yelling, "That's it, Jennings! That's how we do it!"

My teammates, hugging me and slapping me, were going wild. Maurice ran up and gave me a big bear hug. But before I left the field, I went up to that ref, determined to get him to respond.

"Hey, man! You ever see someone score four touchdowns in a row?"

He finally looked at me, and gave me a wink. Thrilled I'd succeeded in penetrating his steely exterior, I gave him a big ol' hug. I knew I wasn't supposed to touch him, but I did it anyway.

As we lined up to shake hands with the Bees, I noticed the little kids who'd been playing along the fence at the edge of the field. I was once that little kid imagining that I was my older brother, when he was playing for Jefferson Forest. Suddenly I was seeing little kids playing and pretending to be me. That blew me away.

Speedy was standing there in line with his hands on his hips, shaking his head.

"Look at you," he said, beaming, "looking like a shining star!"

A line of Brookville players streamed past, saying "Good game," "Good game," "Good game."

When I passed their running back, he looked at me with respect and said, "Man, you killed it out there today."

That was cool to hear.

In the swirl of activity on the field, a news reporter ran up to me and said, "Rashad . . ."

I turned around to find a huge camera in my face, with a bright light shining in my eyes and a microphone extended in my direction. I was never interviewed before and I had no idea what to say.

The reporter asked, "Rashad, where did you come from? You've never played and we don't even have you on our list. We've never spoken to you before, but today you became a legend. You played fourteen total plays, and scored four touchdowns. How does it feel?"

Still feeling like they were talking to the wrong guy, I said, "I don't know . . . uh . . . it feels great, I guess. . . . Uh . . ."

Trying to throw me a bone, the reporter offered another question.

"So how does it feel to end Brookville's season? I know

Photo courtesy of the author

I loved football from a very young age!

Photo courtesy of the author

Photo courtesy of the author

Featured in the church
calendar, March 1992.

Me with my dad and brothers.

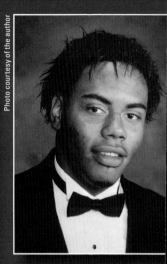

Photo courtesy of the author

Me and my cousins at Grandma's house on Christmas.

Photo courtesy of the author

High School Senior portrait.

Photo courtesy of the author

Jennings family portrait around Thanksgiving.

Playing for the University of Pittsburgh Panthers, 2005.

Hitting the gym at Liberty.

Praying before a game as a member of the
Jacksonville Jaguars, my first NFL team!

Part of my elaborate
pre-game warmup

Running in for a touchdown, 2013.

Copyright 2016 New York Giants Football, Inc.

Copyright 2016 New York Giants Football, Inc.

Bennett Cohen

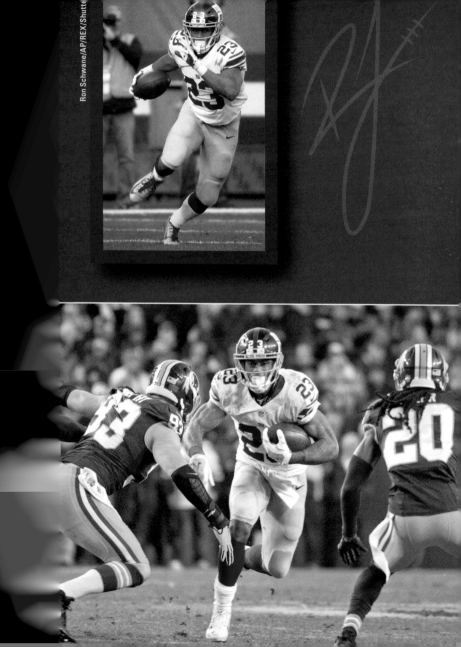

Ron Schwane/AP/REX/Shutt

ABC via Getty Images

ABC via Getty Images

Dancing to "Unconditionally,"
dedicated to my dad.

ABC via Getty Images

We won!

Michelle Burton

Speaking to students in L.A.

Michelle Burton

With students at Bright Star Secondary
Charter Academy.

you don't get to move on to the playoffs, but this has got to be a bittersweet way for you to finish."

"Yeah . . ." I stammered, "bittersweet."

The next thought that passed through my mind was Bit-O-Honey candy, almond bits in a honey-flavored taffy.

Should I mention that?

Luckily, at that moment, one of my teammates came to save me.

"Come on, Shad," he coaxed. "Come celebrate!"

In the locker room, everyone was giving each other high fives, proud that we ended the season the right way. Coach rallied everyone together, "Come on, men, bring it in."

He looked around at us. "Y'all fought. You stayed in the game. You never gave up." Then he paused, and said, "But boy . . . what about that Jennings? Where is he?"

All the guys cheered and when I stood up, Coach handed me the game ball, a huge honor for anyone, but especially for a guy like me.

As I was leaving the locker room to go see my family, there was someone waiting for me. "Rashad," the man said. "Your name's Rashad, right?"

I looked up and saw the white Tennessee logo stitched across his orange golf shirt. I nodded, surprised. This was the Tennessee scout who came to see Quincy. What was he doing talking to me?

"Rashad, I couldn't help but notice you tonight."

I couldn't believe this was happening.

"So tell me, son," he continued, "how are your grades?"

Uh-oh. Almost immediately, I deflated like a pin-pricked balloon.

"I have a . . ." I hedged.

Leaning in closer to hear me better, the scout looked politely puzzled.

I raised my voice a little bit and said, "Uh . . . I have a point six."

"A point six what?"

Not proud of it, I said, "A point six GPA." Then I looked down at the ground, ashamed.

The scout burst out laughing. "You gotta *try* to do something like that!"

I didn't know what to say. All I could do was shrug my shoulders.

"Listen, son, you have potential," the scout said kindly. "Get your grades right, because you could play at the next level."

There they were. The three magic words I'd wanted to hear my whole life. For the first time in my entire life—outside of people like my mom and brothers who I expected to support me—I heard somebody say, "You have potential." That confirmation, coming not only from someone who wasn't obligated to support me, but also from someone with an awful lot of credibility, felt amazing. From the moment the words left his lips, they were carved in my heart. I would cling to them in the months and years to come.

After the scout walked off, I started crying. I was happy, exhausted, and overwhelmed, not just with what had happened that night, but with what my future could be. I hurried out onto the field to look for my family. I had to tell Mom what had happened.

As I scanned the crowd for my mom, Coach grabbed his clipboard from the bench and said, "Rashad, we're going to have plans for you next year!"

"Thanks, Coach," I said, more than a little surprised. Proving myself to my coach felt just as good as hearing those three magic words from the scout.

When I finally saw Mom, I noticed that Butch and Bryan were still there with her. They knew I hadn't seen a minute of playing time all season and would probably have been on the bench this game too, but they were both determined to support their brother and came anyway. Butch and Bryan were both friends with Wayne Lance, who also came with them. He was the head coach at the private school in town where Butch and Bryan had been coaching that year—Lynchburg Christian Academy.

When we all met up, my brothers were raving. Mom, tickled to death, reached around my big body to give me a huge hug. With the biggest smile she told me how my brothers had acted during the game.

"Lord," she exclaimed, "they were excited. When you made that first touchdown, Butch jumped the fence! The security guard had to tell him to get back up in the stands. Your brothers were shouting and hugging and laughing! I'm so proud of you, baby."

It was such a sweet moment for our family. I wish my dad had been there to share it.

Butch's Instructions

Two years earlier, when I was in ninth grade, Butch had been living and ministering in Raleigh, North Carolina, when a visiting preacher had spoken a word of prophecy to him. Butch received it as God's word to him.

"Butch," the preacher had said, "you need to go back and cover your brother as a mentor, like a father would. Your brother has NFL written all over him; together, you will do great things."

Butch knew that "covering" meant supporting and providing an extra layer of protection and guidance. Because Bryan was in transition from NFL teams, Butch's first thought was, "Bryan! Well, that makes sense. He needs me."

The pastor who spoke the word to Butch crossed paths with him after the service and clarified, "Young man, it's not the brother you're thinking of—you have a younger brother. I hear God saying it's him that needs you."

Butch was shocked. What was this guy talking about?

Rashad? He's only fifteen? What great things is he going to do? All that knucklehead does is play video games, joke around, and chill with his boys! Lord, he's got food and candy wrappers stashed under his bed. Are you sure?

I thought the same thing when Butch came home and called a meeting to share the prophecy with our family. *God had spoken to him about me?*

Butch had no idea what the Lord had in store for me but, as a man of faith, he was excited about whatever it was.

In fact, it's the reason he moved back to Lynchburg. Butch wanted me to live with him and his family so that he could train me like a real father would, but Mom wasn't having that. So throughout my high school years, while I continued to live with my folks, Butch supported and mentored me.

Although I hadn't heard God's voice in the same way Butch had, I was really clear that God was with me, just like he was with Butch. I knew God loved me and had good plans for me. And I even believed God was the one who'd given me the drive to work my tail off until the moment of opportunity came. I was learning that God leads, prepares, and speaks to all of us differently.

As my family piled into Mom's car, I was still buzzing with excitement about the amazing game I'd just played.

I had no idea that it would also be my last game at Jefferson Forest.

CHAPTER 8

A SECOND CHANCE

Guess what!?" I burst out, from the backseat where I was sitting with Butch.

I told them about the Tennessee scout, and then added, "And Coach said they have big plans for me next year!"

I'd already begun to imagine next year's crowd roaring like the fans had that night. I expected my family to be as fired up as I was. But my brothers' response wasn't anything close to the delight I felt inside.

"I don't know, Shad," Bryan said hesitantly.

As if they had already discussed it, Butch added, "Hasn't that coach been telling you that you were too fat and too slow for the whole season?"

The imaginary fans I'd pictured cheering me on suddenly fell silent. Nodding my head, I felt completely disoriented by the turn in the conversation. *I thought they'd be as excited as I am. Why aren't they? They'd seen me play. Didn't they realize that this was exactly what I'd been dreaming of?*

I hadn't been aware that Butch and Bryan had

reservations about the whole Jefferson Forest situation. My success on the field that night apparently only reinforced their concerns. On top of that, they recognized that because of my poor grades, I wasn't on track to make it to college. Both of them knew I needed a fresh start.

I also didn't know, when I'd hopped in the car with my mom and brothers, that Butch and Bryan had spent the whole game talking amongst themselves about the need to transfer me to Lynchburg Christian Academy (LCA) where they both were coaching.

As we drove home, Butch suggested the possibility of me attending LCA.

I didn't even know where this school was, and honestly, I couldn't imagine playing with any guys other than my boys on the Cavaliers, especially Maurice.

"Doesn't private school cost a ton of money?" I asked.

I leaned forward to see Mom's face to gage her reaction.

"I don't know how much it costs," she admitted, avoiding my anxious gaze by keeping her eyes fixed on the road. "But I do think that if you got some attention there, it might mean a scholarship to college."

Butch had been the first person in our family to go to college, on a football scholarship, and then Bryan. I knew Mom was so proud of them both. But what college was going to take a kid with grades like mine?

Still, the words of that scout—"You could play at the next level"—continued to echo in my mind. His affirmation, along with my brothers' confidence in me, made me want to do whatever I could do to succeed. Still, I was wary of leaving everything I knew—my friends, my teammates, my entire life—behind.

"I don't want to leave Jefferson Forest," I told them. "This is my *team* and these are my *boys*."

I knew Butch and Bryan understood how important a team was.

"But Shad," Butch said gently, "it's not just about the team. This is about you. You *can't* play college ball with the grades you have now, no matter what any scout says. I think you need a fresh start."

Because I hadn't gotten my act together the previous year when I'd taken a break from football, part of me knew he was right. It was the end of November, and when the semester ended in three weeks, I expected my grades to look the same as they had my sophomore and freshman years.

"I really wanna play at Jefferson Forest next year," I pleaded. I couldn't imagine spending my senior year anywhere else. "Just give me a chance."

Considering my request, Butch suggested, "How about this? If your grades go up, you can stay. But if you don't get your grades up, you transfer to LCA."

Trusting that they had my best interest at heart, I agreed. At that moment, I didn't care about my education. All I wanted to do was replay every second of the most amazing game of my life. Thankfully, after that awful idea about switching schools, we returned to talking about the game. I saw Mom grinning as Butch, Bryan, and I reviewed my four touchdowns, going detail by detail like sports announcers. When Mom slowed to a stop in our driveway, we hopped out of the car to celebrate inside.

As we crossed the lawn, Butch shouted, "That's how Jennings boys play!"

I hoped that Dad had heard him.

Transition

To no one's surprise, my grades did not magically improve the second semester of my junior year. And by the time the school year ended, I knew I was headed to Lynchburg Christian Academy, where I'd don the red and white Bulldog uniform.

Though I'd been resistant to the idea at first, I suddenly realized that one of the prayers I prayed when I was much younger—to be closer to my brothers—was actually being answered through this transition. I never dreamed I'd have the opportunity to play for my brothers, and was committed to putting in the work to make them proud.

The only downside to going to LCA was that attending a private school was pricey. To make it possible for me, both Butch and Bryan decided to funnel their coaching salaries into my tuition account, and my parents planned to take out a loan to pay what wasn't covered. I still can't believe my family was ready to move mountains for me like that. It taught me who our family was and how we rolled. I promised myself that if I could ever bless them in a big way, I would.

But achieving the hopes we all had for my future had

placed a burden squarely on me: improving my academics. Butch was the one who suggested I voluntarily repeat my junior year in order to give myself a chance to meet the academic standards required to play football. Although I wasn't thrilled about a fifth year of high school, I knew that plan would give me two more years to boost my abysmal GPA. It also didn't hurt that I'd have two more years to get the chance to play running back.

Go Bulldogs

Butch and Bryan had already spent one year at LCA working alongside the newly appointed head coach Wayne Lance, whipping the program into shape and building a solid foundation. Prior to their arrival the team had won only seven games in three years. When we won our first game, and then the second of the season, we were totally pumped. We tasted what winning felt like, and we wanted more. Coach Lance, Butch, Bryan, and the rest of the staff worked us hard, and slowly we began to win more games.

One day, while the team was working out in the gym, the coach from Liberty University swung by LCA to see the school. I knew he'd attended a few of our games since he was friends with Coach Lance. The two chatted for a while, and then the coach returned to where the guys and I were working. I asked him if it would be all right for me to speak with the college coach. Ever since that scout from Tennessee had encouraged me at the Brookville game, I'd begun to imagine playing at the next level. And I wanted to make sure I was doing everything I could to get there.

"Sure, go talk to him," Coach Lance encouraged me.

Outside of the brief conversation with that Tennessee scout, this was the first conversation I'd had with someone in college ball. I felt nervous as I approached him.

"Hey, Coach," I began. "I'm going into my senior year next year, and wanted to know what you think I need to do to play college football."

He looked me up and down. "You're not going to be playing."

Huh?

"Why not?" I asked, confused. I knew he'd seen a few of our games.

"Because you're not good enough," he said simply.

I was speechless. Not sure how to respond, I walked away and returned to training. The sting of his words lingered with me for days.

If you've ever been evaluated or judged on your performance, whether for a speech, an artistic performance, or for an athletic contest or academic project, the negative comments people make can stick with you. It's the same with family. It can be easy for one person's criticism of you to carry more weight than the love and affirmation of others. And sometimes the negative opinions end up being stickier than the positive ones.

If you let those words have power—*if* you let them get traction in your mind and heart—they can derail your dreams.

I had family, coaches, and even a college scout who believed in me and what I could accomplish. But the curt dismissal by that single coach rang so much louder in my head than the confidence of those I trusted most. Not forever, but for a few days. *If* I had allowed his grim prediction to knock me off course, I probably wouldn't be writing this book today to tell *you* to ignore those negative voices too. I had to choose to let his words, his *opinion*, roll off my back as I continued to hustle to become who I wanted to be.

I'd show him, and everyone, what I could do.

Academics

When I wasn't working on my football game, I was working on my grades. With Butch and Bryan's encouragement, I applied myself to working hard in school, but I still struggled. There was so much ground to cover, so many years of not studying or understanding the material to overcome. Sometimes, the gap between where I was and where I needed to be to get into college felt like an ocean. Even getting all As, which I was far from achieving, wouldn't have boosted my GPA to where it needed to be. I had to do more.

So during the summer before my senior year, and even into the fall, I had to take several summer school classes and nine homeschool classes on top of the regular load of courses I already had. That workload tested the limits of my commitment to realizing my dreams. If I'd known what lay ahead of me when I started, I might never have begun.

But the promise of playing ball for my brothers, and this glimpse I'd had of going on to play at the next level, kept me motivated. While my friends were going fishing and swimming that summer, or working part-time jobs, I was studying. I had no life—school for me was a full-time gig, from 8 a.m. to 8 p.m. every single day. It was hard to focus on conquering years of material, and it was even harder knowing my friends were out having fun without me. Although I didn't feel completely alone—Mom and my brothers were always encouraging me—it was a rough season.

I hadn't failed academically at Jefferson Forest only because I'd been cutting it up as the class clown. My stubborn insistence on always wanting to understand why—*Why history? Am I ever going to need to know this?*—as well as my reading comprehension deficit had both contributed to my struggles. Although I still lived with the learning deficit, I did finally have the answer to my *why*. (Well, I knew why I was working to improve my grades—but I still wasn't convinced I needed to know the date General Lee had thrown his men under the bus!) I was putting in the work so that I could achieve the goals that had been rooted in me since I was a boy. And that was enough to get me through the summer. I was finally motivated, finally taking responsibility for my life.

Razzle Dazzle

The seed of possibility that had been planted in my heart during the Brookville game was beginning to take root and grow. I was working hard in my summer school classes. I'd begun to work out at the YMCA on weekends. And I'd even started to visualize playing college ball and succeeding academically. To make it to that next level, though, I'd need to be seen by someone who could help me get there.

During summer workouts, Coach Lance sent home flyers for a Razzle Dazzle football camp at the University of Pittsburgh. It was an amazing camp, but it cost four hundred and fifty dollars to attend. When I sheepishly handed the flyer to my mom, I honestly didn't know if it was something we could afford. But having had two older sons who'd made it to the NFL, she understood how important these kinds of opportunities were for players to be seen by college coaches. Like she had with school and a million other things, Mom found a way to make the camp possible. And Bryan attended as a coach.

The three-day camp was so fun. The focus of the camp was learning and honing skills, but it was also an opportunity to visit a college, stay in the dorms, and get players psyched to go back home and work hard.

I played quarterback in the Razzle Dazzle game on the second day of camp. After the game, one of Pittsburgh's assistant coaches—who was coaching my team—remarked, "You can *move* for a big guy." He wasn't wrong. When Coach Lance talked about my play, he'd always say, "He's got little man moves in a big man body."

That evening, I was invited to be among a group of seventeen guys, out of the four hundred who were at the camp, who'd work out separately the next day and perform for the coaches and scouts who'd showed up.

The next morning, when they lined us up in the indoor Pittsburgh University training facility, my mind was blown! This was where the magic happened.

Being chosen to be part of that elite group was a big deal, and while I knew it made some guys really nervous, the opportunity just fired me up to prove myself to the coaches and scouts at the camp. I'd been waiting for that moment since peewee league. Finally people were taking notice.

One of the ways players were measured, a test that pro-hopefuls also had to perform at the NFL combine, was running a forty-yard dash. Coaches were looking for players who could demonstrate a powerful burst of speed. As I watched two heats of guys run the forty ahead of mine, I felt anxious. While big men offer a lot to a football team, speed isn't one of the gifts we are known for. Some of the leaner guys could sprint like jackrabbits, and I took a deep breath to calm my nerves.

I lined up with the third group of guys to run the forty. When the gun went off, I started a bit slower than the other players, but ended up finishing strong. As I caught my breath after the run, I noticed the coaches and scouts looking at their stopwatches and talking to each other.

"Hey, Rashad!" one of them yelled. "Do it again."

That's weird. Why do they want me to do it again?

Walking back to the starting line, I lined up and waited for the gun. I exploded from the line and powered through to the finish. Gulping in deep breaths of air, I watched the group of men comparing stopwatches.

One asked, "How much do you weigh?"

"Two sixty-five," I answered.

Another exclaimed, "No way!"

The Pittsburgh assistant coach led us over to a scale, and these guys gathered around as I stood on the scale.

It read 265.8 pounds.

Even though, as a rule, football players need to be big and fast, it's still a rare combo to find those who are *both*. More often, a player will be one or the other.

"Man," the coach from Pitt exclaimed, "I wanna talk to your coach."

I could read the faces of the coaches and scouts and knew they were impressed by my speed. Although I didn't know exactly what would come of it, and despite the fact that no one was being recruited at the camp, it felt great to be noticed. Private high schools in small towns don't get a lot of attention from coaches and scouts. Without the opportunity to have gone to this camp, that Mom made possible with her hard work and penny-pinching, these guys never would have known about me.

At the end of camp, before we loaded back onto the bus to go home, the head coach from Pittsburgh, who'd only come for the last day of camp, pulled me aside.

"Rashad," he said, "we haven't seen your tape yet, but we want to offer you a full scholarship if you come to Pitt."

I was dumbfounded. And also glad he hadn't asked about my grades.

Barely able to speak, I was finally able to spit out two words, "Thank you."

When I got on the bus, I poured out the whole story to Bryan. I called Butch to inform him of the news. Amazed, he told me that a coach making an offer without ever seeing film from a game just *doesn't* happen. My dreams were coming true. I was going to play college ball.

Discipline

Because others saw something in me worth investing in, something clicked inside me and I started investing in myself. I'd believed in my dream for a long time, but that belief had endured more than enough attacks from critics like my dad, some of my coaches, and sometimes even other guys on the team. But now I had something to hold onto—a future with college and football, two things that almost no one but me would have believed possible.

One Saturday morning, after returning from camp, I woke up, put my shorts and T-shirt on, and laced up my running shoes. After stretching, I walked out the front door, and jogged to the street. Heading back out of our neighborhood on Cimarron Road, I started running toward the YMCA, which was about three and a half miles away. I worked out there all day, and when I was done, I ran back home. From that day on, I started running everywhere I went.

Running alone was good for me, because it meant I wasn't comparing myself to others. It was like playing an individual sport for the first time, which meant I needed to be even more disciplined than when I had a team or coach to cheer—or goad—me on. While I felt like I was going to *die* on day one, gradually, I began to get stronger. I'd run until I couldn't run anymore, then I'd pull my inhaler out of my shorts and use it to open my airway. Although my doctors had advised against strenuous activity, I could sense improvement and felt like my lungs were getting stronger.

Around that time, I also decided it was time to get serious about nutrition. I'd always known that if I wanted to shed pounds I should change my diet and exercise. But for some reason, I just hadn't done it. So one day I decided to conduct a food experiment.

On the kitchen counter, I set out a McDonald's burger and fries that I'd brought home and put in the fridge the night before. I also poured a glass of milk and laid out one slice of cheese. This, one of my favorite dinners when out with my friends, was meal #1. Beside it, I laid out meal #2: a head of lettuce, a lean chicken breast, a banana, and a glass of water.

My mom, a self-professed neat freak, was horrified.

"Boy, if you don't clean that mess up . . ."

"Trust me, Mom," I told her. "I'm doing an experiment. I'm going to leave them out for three days and see what happens."

Though she hated messes, and also hated to waste food,

Mom loved me. So she let me keep my little mad scientist experiment.

After three days, I reviewed the results. The burger had thickened and was hard as a rock. The milk stunk. I put meal number one in a bowl and pushed it toward the wall. Then, I surveyed meal #2. The chicken was a little stiffer than it had been three days earlier, but everything else seemed fine. I placed meal #2 in a separate bowl, stirred it up, and left it on the counter. As time passed, I could see that the second meal eventually broke down and began to decay, but without the nasty smells and rot I'd observed in the first one.

From that day on, I aimed to only eat foods that would deteriorate naturally when left alone. I cut out fast foods and committed to making healthy choices. A typical meal for me included a chicken breast, rice, broccoli, and a salad. As a result of my new discipline, both with exercising and eating right, I lost thirty-five pounds and improved my forty-yard dash time by two-tenths of a second.

I was finally getting my act together. I was working hard to complete my summer school classes. I was working out. I'd begun to eat right. I was determined to achieve my dream, and I was finally taking the steps I needed to take to make it a reality. With determination and hard work, I made progress academically and physically.

When you set your mind to achieve your goals, you don't have to make all the changes at once. I put in the effort on academics. Then physical training. Then diet. By setting your mind to meeting smaller goals, you'll eventually reach the big ones.

And I can't stress enough the importance of a strong support system. People in your corner who will encourage you, believe in you, and even sacrifice for you are precious gifts. When I argued with Butch and Bryan about switching schools from Jefferson Forest, I had no idea what my first year at Lynchburg Christian would bring. But if I could have seen where I would end up as I began my senior year, I would have saved my breath.

I was finally on my way to success, and nothing could stop me.

CHAPTER 9

THE BIG RUN

Because I was so young when my brothers left for college, I missed having the experience of sharing a home with them for any length of time. Yeah, I annoyed them like little brothers do, like when I butted in on Bryan's relationship with Pam, but I didn't have the opportunity to really *know* them. So knowing that I would be working with them at LCA, I felt like I would get an awesome opportunity to spend time with them.

Growing up, I was constantly living in the shadow of two brothers who'd not only gone to college, but had both played in the NFL. When I was still at Jefferson Forest, I couldn't walk down the hall without being reminded of the awards Bryan had won and records he'd broken in football, basketball, and track. Whenever I would point to the trophy case and brag—"That's my brother!"—I would either get the side-eye or someone would come right out and remind me of my lack of athletic achievement. "So what happened to you?" they'd ask. Once I transferred to LCA, not only did I have a chance to forge my own path, but I got to do it with my brothers by my side.

Even though my brothers expected me to do my best at whatever I tried, they'd never pressured me to play football and never assumed my path would look just like theirs. When I was given the opportunity to play for them, I wanted to prove to them that I was serious about making the changes I needed to make for my future.

I wanted to make them proud.

Going the Distance

One Saturday morning, Mom was out at the grocery store and Dad was in his bedroom smoking. I was suited up in my running clothes. I wore a T-shirt with cutoff sleeves, my blue basketball shorts, and a pair of running shoes. Strapping my MP3 player to my upper arm, I stepped out onto the front steps.

I jogged to the end of our driveway, and then took a left on Cimarron Road to head out of our neighborhood. Breaking Benjamins were on the playlist that would propel me through the longest run I had attempted to date. I hadn't told anyone what I was up to, because *talking about* commitment is worth little, but *demonstrating* commitment is worth everything.

I jogged four miles in the direction of the YMCA, the route I ran every weekend, but the Y wasn't my destination. Butch and his family were living in Lynchburg, and I'd made up my mind that I'd run to see him that morning.

It was 12.6 miles from my house.

Instead of turning down Enterprise Drive, toward the YMCA, I headed to Lynchburg, sweat pouring off my forehead. When I reached what I estimated to be the halfway point, the skies opened up and it began to rain. Though breathing was difficult, I was a lot healthier since I'd been working out regularly. And the rain felt great. On the second half of the run, my skin began to chafe from the damp clothing, but I kept going.

When I set off on my "big run," I had no way of knowing whether I had what it took physically to keep going for a dozen miles. But what I did have was determination and vision. Butch had been teaching me to visualize myself in situations that matched where I wanted to be in the future.

For instance, during one of our games (this was after I'd verbally committed to go to Pitt), he barked in my face, "Who are you playing against?!" Obviously, we were playing the other school out on the field—Norcross. When I said so, he retorted, "No! It's your first game of the season, who are you playing against?!" At first, I thought he'd lost his mind! But after a moment, I offered the name of Pitt's first opponent of the following year.

"Notre Dame?" I guessed.

"Yes!" he bellowed. "Notre Dame!"

The ferocity, enthusiasm, and volume were *classic* Butch.

"And who do you play next week?" he asked.

Since my guess was as good as his, and since there were

two teams of players on the field waiting to resume the game, I guessed, "Ohio?"

"That's right!" he yelled. "Ohio! Now get out there!"

By visualizing myself playing against these football greats, Butch was firing me up to play at the next level. That way, when I stepped back out on the field and saw nothing but mere mortal high school players, I'd crushed them.

So throughout my run, I never saw myself stopping until I got to Butch's house. I didn't imagine going to work out at the Y, like I did most Saturdays. I only pictured myself showing up at Butch's, ringing the doorbell, and coolly stepping inside.

Surprise!

Miles and miles later, I was gulping in oxygen when I rang Butch's doorbell. Beads of rain-diluted sweat fell onto his porch as I drank in the damp air. After about a minute, Butch answered the door. His face lit up when he saw me.

"Hey, Shad!"

Suddenly, his gaze moved past me and toward his driveway, as if searching for our mother's car.

"Where's Ma?" he asked.

I grinned as I watched him try to put all the pieces together.

"She's not here," I told him. "I ran."

Butch craned his neck further to see if her car might be parked a few houses down.

"Nah, man, don't play," he pressed. "Where is she?"

The brutal half-marathon was worth it to me, if only for the opportunity to watch Butch figure it all out.

"Really," I explained, "I ran here."

Butch's eyes grew wide.

"Man, come on in!" he ordered. "Get some water!"

While I put some ice into the biggest cup I could find in Butch's kitchen, I heard him calling Bryan.

"Bryan," he began, "did you give Shad a ride to my house?"

Silence.

"Nah, he's here," Butch announced, "and he says he *ran* here from home!"

The pride and delight in his voice thrilled me.

After he hung up with Bryan, Butch invited me to sit down with him at the kitchen table.

Butch pummeled me with questions about the workouts I was doing, trying to figure out how I'd built my strength and stamina to run what amounted to almost a half marathon. Because I could tell my brother was really interested, I ended up sharing a little more than I did in our typical conversations. I admitted that—although I covered it up with my big smile and goofiness—I was embarrassed by my weight, and the acne and eczema that had started to appear.

"Man," he asked, "is that why you're always wearing those clothes?"

I knew what he meant. Although I didn't quite need the sizes I bought, I was wearing size 5X shirts and 4X pants. Honestly, I think they were my shell. They protected me from feeling like others could see right through my happy façade.

"Hey," I came back defensively, "that's my style!"

But even as I was saying it, I knew Butch was right.

"Well . . . maybe . . ." I admitted.

"You're good, Shad," he encouraged me. "And I believe in you, no matter what size you are."

The support and encouragement I'd received from Butch and Bryan throughout the previous year and a half convinced me that he meant it. I knew they wanted me to be all I could be physically, academically, and even spiritually. And Butch was committed to his role as my spiritual mentor. So whenever he could help me understand how much God cared for me, he seized the opportunity.

Butch continued, "Mark tells a story of a dad who takes his boy to Jesus because that boy was being tormented by evil spirits."

Always a smart aleck, I interrupted, "You're not saying I'm possessed, are you?"

"Shad, pay attention," he coaxed. "When the spirit in the boy saw Jesus, it threw the boy to the ground in a fit. The dad says to Jesus, 'If you can do anything, take pity on us and help us.'"

"Help 'em, Lord!" I chimed in playfully.

Butch ignored me and continued, "Jesus told the dad, 'Everything is possible for one who believes.'"

"What are you saying to me?" I asked Butch, knowing that his Bible stories always had a point.

"I'm saying, Shad, that anything is possible. I've seen you hustling to get your grades right, and now I see you working to get fit. I know God has a good plan for you, and I see you putting in the work to do your part. I'm proud of you, Shad."

His affirmation felt great.

"Hey, thanks, man," I said, finally being serious. "That means a lot."

Pondering

For weeks after that day, I kept thinking about the story Butch told me. I'd repeat the mantra, "Everything is possible for one who believes." I always knew God was watching over me, and I did believe that he could help me do anything.

But the part of the story that really landed in my heart was that the dad brought his boy to Jesus. Although I wished my dad was like that, like a few of the fathers I saw each week with their families in church, he just wasn't. It didn't seem to me like Dad wanted to be a godly man, and he certainly didn't seem very interested in me.

But as I thought about the ways Butch and Bryan had been taking care of me during my final two years of high school—coaching me, mentoring me, and helping to pay for my tuition—I saw in them a glimpse of that dad who brought his son to Jesus. They didn't force me to go to church or give me religious lectures, but the way they lived their lives showed me what it looked like to be a man who trusts God. At this point, it had been about six years since I'd vowed that I would not grow up to be like Dad. But I knew without a doubt I *did* want to grow up to be like my brothers. These two men, one in his early thirties and the other his late twenties, had filled that void by loving me the way a father is supposed to love a son.

Having a father who shows you what God's love is like is one of the important "ifs" in life. And while I know that no father is perfect, some human fathers do a better job than others of showing their children what God's love is like. *If* you haven't had a father who has a heart for God—or for you—I encourage you to find men or women who can reflect that for you. Maybe, like me, they'll be men or women in your family. Or maybe there's a coach, a teacher, or a pastor whom you admire and respect. God can use these people to show the great love he has for you.

He did it for me.

Learning to Lead

One of the things I've learned is that God not only wants to bless us with men and women in our lives who care for us the way Butch and Bryan cared for me, he wants us to *be* that kind of person as well. For some, that may mean becoming a loving parent. Or it might mean becoming the kind of coach—or teacher, or police officer, or businessperson, or pastor—who takes care of others.

But I don't think that investing in others is something that's just for the future. God gives us gifts to encourage and inspire others right where we are. I tried to do that on and off the field. I'd push my teammates to put in the work we needed to be successful. When my friends asked for it, I offered advice or opinions on dating and partying. When I'd see little kids playing on the side of the field at the high school games, I'd encourage them to keep hustling.

There might even be a younger person you can impact living under your own roof. Although I didn't have one, believe me, I get how annoying younger siblings can be sometimes. I *was* that kid! But I want you to understand that the impact you have on siblings, or younger kids in your neighborhood or church, is huge. They look up to you whether you realize it or not. And when you take an interest in them, notice their gifts, and inspire them to be the best they can be, it can make a big difference in their lives. Your encouragement and involvement could help that kid who struggles between giving up—because they think they're too stupid, too fat, or just not enough—and choosing to face their challenges and find success.

You're never too old or too young, too popular or too weird, too powerful or too weak to help someone else.

CHAPTER 10

LEAVING THE NEST

Making it to college had seemed like such a remote possibility when my GPA at Jefferson Forest High was 0.6. But I'd worked hard at LCA. When I graduated, I'd scored more touchdowns than any other player in the school's history. And once I started working my tail off academically, it really started to pay off too. Thanks to all the summer school and homeschool classes I took, I got my GPA high enough to go to college and play ball. I received scholarship offers from both Pitt and VA Tech.

I chose Pitt.

Unfortunately, my improved academic standing didn't happen soon enough for me to start school in the fall. So I had to stand by and watch as my friends went off to play college ball. Rather than seeing that as an obstacle, I seized it as an opportunity. I continued to train from home so that when I arrived on campus in January, I would be as lean, fast, and strong as I could be.

But as the fall went on, I began to feel nervous. *Would I*

get to see playing time? Would I miss home? Would I survive academically?

That last one was a biggie. In November and December, I began badgering Butch and Bryan with questions about academics, team study hall, grades, and homework. If I struggled through high school, how on earth was I supposed to thrive in college classes? Both Butch and Bryan admitted that college coursework would demand disciplined effort, but they also told me they believed I could do it. They'd seen my drive to succeed, and believed that I had what it took to succeed in college as well as football. During that season when I felt so nervous about beginning school, I leaned into their confidence.

The night before I left for college, I tried a technique Butch taught me. Instead of worrying about the future, I closed my eyes and visualized myself crossing the stage at Pitt's graduation ceremony. Seeing myself in a black cap and gown fueled my commitment to keep doing whatever it took to realize the dreams I had for my life.

The morning Mom drove me to Pittsburgh, I looked in the mirror at my newly toned body. In September, I'd weighed in at 265, a few pounds below what I was when the coaches at Pitt saw me at camp after my junior year. Stepping on the scale four months later, I watched the digital numbers rise and fall as the scale calculated my weight, finally slowing to a stop at 245 pounds. Because I knew I'd added muscle mass during those months of intense conditioning, it meant I'd lost more than twenty pounds of excess fat. Stepping off the scale and grabbing the last of my bags from my room, I felt like it was time.

I was ready.

Life at Pitt

When I arrived on campus, my good friend Tyler, from LCA, introduced me to the guys on the team. They'd been working together all season and didn't know anything about this new player. But Tyler helped to smooth that transition for all of us.

Starting college in January worked well for me. It gave me the spring semester before training started in June to figure out how to be a college student and get my academics in order! I took advantage of all the resources available to help me succeed, including attending study hall for athletes. There was no way I was going to miss the ten hours of study hall that was required for first-year players. Players who didn't complete those hours had to roll their bodies— sideways, like a hot dog—down all one hundred yards of the football field. Our coaches were serious about our education, not just our athleticism. Only one player assigned the task that year was able to do it without vomiting before the end of the roll. The threat of that consequence was pretty powerful motivation to show up. Not only did I do *15* hours of study hall a week, I set myself up to graduate with a double-major in just three years. By the end of my first semester, I had attained a 3.5 GPA.

As I started to get grades back from my professors, I

realized, to my surprise, that I really could succeed in a competitive academic world. My brothers and mother had been right, my experience at LCA prepared me well for that first year of college. Teachers and coaches at LCA had been committed to not giving athletes special treatment, and my brothers were there to double down on that commitment! As a result, I never missed a class at LCA.

My fears about failing in college the way I did at Jefferson Forest were slowly put to rest as I discovered I could do the work that was expected of me, and do it *well*! In fact, I won a freshman writing award that year for the best essay.

The first day of English class, the professor came in and told us that our first major assignment for the class would be a fifteen-page paper in MLA format, and we could write about anything we wanted. Always pushing to challenge status quo and test limits, I decided that since I could write about anything, I was going to devote a 15-page paper to the topic of "nothing." To my surprise, writing 15 pages about "nothing"—both the presence of nothing and the absence of nothing—was actually a really fun experiment for my brain, as I enjoyed abstract thinking. Thankfully, my teacher agreed!

The irony of it all is that back in high school, I got all Fs no matter how hard I tried. But in college, writing a paper about "nothing" earned me an A and a writer of the year award.

I dreamed of playing college ball, but in my wildest dreams I never once imagined receiving an academic award. I felt really proud of that success.

The Team

We took a four-week break after school ended in the spring, then the team started summer workouts in June. It had been 18 months since the end of my senior year season, and I was eager to play ball again. I spent all those months conditioning, and I was ready to show the results of my hard work on the field.

During those workouts, I gave everything I had, and even when the other players left for the evening, I stayed and kept working. As the other players dispersed to hit the locker room or hustled away to make it to the dining hall, my individual practice would begin. I ran sprints, rehearsed drills, and went to the weight room to lift extra weight. I didn't believe that conditioning was a one-size-fits-all endeavor, so it made sense that we should all practice in our own way. Like the hardheaded kid I was in high school, I didn't depend on coaches or trainers to plan every aspect of my training. I knew I needed to do more than was required if I wanted to be the best I could be. This was the good side of being stubborn!

The reason I kept hustling was because I knew exactly *why* I was doing it. I could visualize the end game—playing in the NFL—and that *why* is what drove me. That *why* motivated every lift, every run, every workout, and every meal.

When you know your *why*—for buckling down in school, for honing your craft, for developing a new skill, or for conditioning your body—you've discovered a motivation that can *move* you when you don't feel like moving anymore. As you hold in your mind a picture of the goal you're after, you have a reason for showing up early, giving your all, and staying late. Whether anyone else notices, that *why* is what helps you keep making the right choices—even the hard ones.

And even though you're doing it to become the best you can be, sometimes that extra effort *will* be noticed! When 109 players trickle off the field after practice, and one player stays to keep working, coaches *notice*. Mine did.

During our first game of the season, the previous year's starting running back was still listed as a starter on the roster. The new coaching staff had used the previous season's starting team as the default roster to begin our new year. But because I'd been getting stronger and faster, I was getting closer and closer to edging out the starting senior running back. When we were watching game film the week after that first game—the game Butch had had me visualize almost two years earlier—we saw that the starting back missed pass protection. Then he missed it again.

The coach barked at him, "Who are you supposed to block?"

The starting back guessed the wrong player.

Turning to me, the coach demanded, "Jennings, who are you supposed to block?!"

I correctly identified the opposing player the starting running back should have blocked. Two weeks later I was starting as running back. And that year I became one of only four freshmen at Pitt to have ever started as a running back—also on that list was the great Tony Dorsett, the 1976 Heisman Trophy winner and NFL Hall-of-Famer.

The Jacket

In February, as I began my third semester at Pitt, Tyler and I drove the six hours home for the long Presidents' Day weekend. I felt excited because I had something I was really psyched to share with Dad. Although he was never very open with his emotion, I still hoped he would celebrate the great news with me.

When Tyler dropped me off at home, Mom was in the kitchen preparing dinner and Dad was watching television in the living room. Mom, who heard the front door open, dashed out of the kitchen and gave me a big hug. Without turning his head from the screen, Dad offered an obligatory, "Hey, Shad."

My heart raced with anticipation as I pulled a carefully folded jacket out of my duffle bag and held it up for him to see. The letterman's jacket had a black felted body and gold leather sleeves, with a proud golden "P" stitched onto the chest.

"Dad," I burst out. "Look, I got a letterman's jacket!"

Before he'd entered the service, my dad had earned a scholarship to play college football, so I knew he'd understand how much it meant.

"Oh, Shad," Mom said, beaming. "That's fantastic!"

Dad was unresponsive.

Then, glancing briefly at my prize, he asked, "So?"

My heart sunk. I felt my face flush as shame washed over me. *Why had I thought he would care?*

Mom, trying to ease the awkward tension, continued to gush, "Baby, that's so wonderful. We're so proud of you!"

She said "we," but it was crystal clear that she didn't speak for Dad.

Unable to hide my disappointment, I kept looking toward Dad.

Feeling my gaze, he demanded, "So, what you want me to do?"

Hoping to convey the significance of the honor I was awarded at a football banquet at school a few weeks earlier, I kept talking.

"Only four freshmen got one this year," I explained.

My mom quietly rubbed my back, as if her silent support could compensate for his lack of affection.

"So?" he answered bluntly, adding, "you still ain't in the league."

I was nineteen years old, and instead of congratulating me for the honor I had earned at school, all he could do was point out the fact that I hadn't been drafted to the NFL.

I truly felt that nothing I did would ever be good enough for him. And I wanted so badly to prove myself to him, to have him acknowledge all I had accomplished. If he only knew what his words were doing to me, I wondered if he would have acted differently. How could a father you love not be proud of you?

"Come on, Shaddy Rock," Mom coaxed me. "Let's go hang it up in your closet. It's just beautiful."

I'd thought so too. But suddenly the jacket seemed unimportant. With a hurting heart, I threw it over my duffle bag, grabbed my things, and followed Mom to my room.

The Call

Maybe you think I'm crazy for holding out for my dad's approval. Maybe you have a dad exactly like that. Either way, I eventually shook off the disappointment like I always did. I had to keep moving—I wanted to finish the semester strong, and I couldn't let his negativity hold me back.

But about a month after I returned to school after that visit, I got a call from Mom.

Recognizing her number, I answered my phone enthusiastically, "Hi, Mom!"

"Hi, baby," she responded, her voice tight and worried.

I knew something was wrong.

"Mom, what is it?" I asked. "Are you okay?"

"I am, Shad, but Dad isn't."

"What's going on?" I demanded.

"Well," she began, "his diabetes has gotten worse."

I knew that Dad had lost a toe to diabetes and was using a walker to get around. *Had it gotten worse than that?*

With a quiver in her voice, Mom continued, "The doctors need to amputate his leg."

I was sitting alone in my dorm room when I got this news. I felt like my heart had stopped.

I fought back tears.

"Mom," I offered, "I'm so sorry! How's Dad?"

I almost didn't want to ask.

"You know your father . . ." she began, before her voice trailed off.

I assumed her vague response meant what I feared: angry ugly words, drinking too much, stress smoking. Mom never wanted to say an unkind word about anyone, and it always amazed me that she could hold her tongue when it came to my father. She was, and is, the strongest person I know.

"Do Butch and Bryan know?" I asked.

"Yes, they've known for a few months that this was a possibility."

Though I didn't like it, my family still treated me as the baby, wanting to protect me from this hard news.

"When is it happening?" I asked.

"His surgery is scheduled for next week," she said. "But don't you worry about it. Butch and Bryan are here."

"No, I'm coming home," I said, impulsively.

"You need to focus on school," she chided. "I know finals are coming up, and you need to stay focused. That's why I didn't want to mention it to you."

"Mom, this is a really big deal. You're going to need help. I'm coming home."

She tried to resist, but my hardheadedness was no match for her.

"Mom, I've gotta go, but we'll talk soon," I promised. "I love you, Mom. And I'll be praying for you and Dad."

"Sweetie, I don't want you to worry about this," she protested.

"Mom, I got you."

"I know, baby," she finally conceded. "I love you, Shaddy Rock."

"I love you, too, Mom."

After we hung up, I began to strategize how I could get home to help my parents.

Without Support

I wasn't interested in just going home to help my mom for a week. I wanted to transfer schools so that I could be closer to home to help my parents on a regular basis. I loved playing for Pitt, but because my parents had taken care of me for nineteen years, I'd gladly sacrifice three for them. Whether that meant physically helping to care for Dad or lending emotional support to Mom, I knew I needed to be home.

But no one in my family—not Mom, Butch, or Bryan— was having it. My family believed that God had plans for me that included the NFL, and to leave Pitt would be like throwing those dreams away. While there was a slim chance I could still make it to the league, I knew I'd be sacrificing my best chances if I left Pitt.

After I spoke with Mom, I went directly to my coach to explain the situation. Although he didn't want to lose me, he understood my family situation and assured me that he was willing to release my papers and grant me a hardship transfer.

All I needed was to find another school, near home, where I could play football.

During my next visit home, Butch, Bryan, and I discussed it. Butch suggested I consider playing for Liberty.

I chuckled, "Nah, I don't think so, man!"

I had no interest in playing for the coach who'd once told me I'd never play in college.

But Butch, who was working in the Center for Multicultural Enrichment at Liberty University, had heard that Liberty was looking at one of the coaches at UVA, Coach Rocco, to be their next head football coach. Bryan, who knew that if I played for a Division I school I'd be forced to sit out a season, encouraged me to consider it. Because I respected my brothers, I began to entertain the possibility.

When Butch called Coach Rocco and didn't get a response, he decided we were going to take a road trip to UVA. Convincing the receptionist in the athletic department that we were recruits, we talked our way into his office. When Butch explained our situation, Coach Rocco admitted that he had gotten Butch's message, and apologized for not returning his call.

He explained, "I was excited to get your call. However, I believe in doing things the right way. I'm still wrapping things up here and wanted to honor UVA by finishing strong."

That response showed me he was a man of integrity, and Butch and I were both impressed. We briefly discussed the possibility of doing great things together at Liberty. It was like the pieces of my puzzle were starting to come together, and I could finally see a clear picture emerging.

As we were driving back home that evening, I got an idea. Thirteen guys I'd known from Jefferson Forest and LCA had gone on to play Division I football. Over the course of the next week, I called them one by one, turning on all my charm to convince them to come play at Liberty with me.

Ultimately, the decision to play at Liberty wasn't a difficult one for me, because I knew exactly *why* I was doing it. Supporting my family was something I had to do. And because I never lost sight of that *why*, I never regretted transferring schools.

This was another one of those *if* moments, one of the most important ones of my life. *If* I'd stayed at Pitt, I would have enjoyed plenty of advantages. But *if* I'd made that decision, I would have sacrificed what mattered most to me: caring for my family.

Some of the decisions you'll make won't be popular with everyone. That was certainly true for me in this case! But if you can hang on to the *why* that's driving you, you'll have the motivation you need to help you follow through with the commitments you make, especially when they require sacrifice.

By the time I was suiting up for the first game of Liberty's season, in the fall of 2006, seven of those old friends who'd played ball with me in high school were by my side. The hometown boys were coming back to do some good on the gridiron.

CHAPTER 11

COMING HOME

The week before Liberty's season began, the school's chancellor, Jerry Falwell, who everyone on campus called "Doc," called me into his office. Sitting in the hallway, waiting to be invited in, I felt nervous. *Was I in trouble?* I hadn't done anything wrong, but I'd learned in high school that I could get in trouble for stuff I hadn't even done!

When his secretary ushered me in to see Doc, I glanced around the beautiful wood-paneled office. It was lined with bookshelves, and on the wall was a huge vision map showing how Doc dreamed Liberty University's campus would look one day.

As Doc stood up from the leather chair behind his desk, I reached across and shook his hand.

"Great to see you again, Rashad," he began.

Because my high school had played on Liberty's field, Doc remembered me.

"Thank you. It's great to see you, sir," I replied.

"Have a seat," he encouraged me, pointing to a chair.

I sat down and waited for the axe to fall.

"Rashad," he began, "I'm so excited you decided to come back to Liberty."

Phew! It didn't seem like I was in trouble.

"I'm glad to be here," I said.

I'd been working out with the team for two months, and was excited about what we might do. But we both knew there was a lot of work ahead. Liberty had won only one game the previous season, and had won *none* against our opponents in the Big South conference.

I'd heard that Dr. Falwell was a big football fan, and that sometimes while preaching a sermon, he'd go on tangents about football.

"Rashad," he said, looking me right in the eyes, "I know that you are going to be the person to help turn this program around. I know you're going to elevate our level of play to the point where we will be able to play Notre Dame one day."

Gulp. No pressure there. Notre Dame was just a Division I school with 11 national titles. *No problem, Doc.* And yet when someone challenged me to do what seemed impossible, it only fueled my fire.

He wasn't done.

"There's no doubt in my mind that you will lay the groundwork for us to *beat* Notre Dame one day."

I thought *I* was a dreamer, but this man took the cake. If he could dream it, though, then so could I.

Sobered, I held his gaze. "I accept the challenge."

We shot the breeze about football for a few minutes before I had to leave for practice.

I had a lot of work to do.

The Why

The team rallied together, and after winning our first game of the season, at home against St. Paul, the Liberty Flames went on to have a winning season. We were on our way to becoming the successful program Doc believed we could be and we'd go on to achieve even more the next two years.

While I loved playing at Liberty, I never lost sight of the reason I'd returned to Lynchburg. I went home every Sunday to be with my family and would also visit a few times during the week. Sometimes I'd help Dad in and out of their accessible van, and other times we just hung out and watched a game together, always betting on the outcome and talking trash the whole game. I'd crack jokes with him and make sure he had whatever he needed. One of those "needs" even became a joke between us.

When I was growing up, if I was home during the late morning in the summer, Dad would bark, "Rashad, go check the mail!" Because we lived in a subdivision in a rural area, that order meant a long walk to the street to peek in the mailbox where the mail may or may not have been delivered. If he could have just waited until three or four o'clock, we would have been guaranteed a full mailbox, but for some reason he didn't want our bills and junk mail getting stale out there. So when I started visiting him while at Liberty, no matter what time of day it was, I'd always play with him, asking, "Dad, you want me to go check the mail?" At first it just irritated him, but after a while, I'd catch a little grin on his face. Against his will, he was starting to soften.

Gradually, I began to see our relationship change. Dad never said anything out loud, but I started to sense his appreciation. Although he'd dismissed my accomplishments at Pitt, he knew I'd been on the path of success, and he knew the reason I'd come back to a smaller school was because I wanted to be there for him. I chose to be there for someone who didn't encourage me, or even take an interest in me in the past. I chose to do this for someone who acted like he didn't believe in me.

I believe the weight of that reality began to eat at him. Despite years of disregard and even disrespect, I never cursed Dad. I never hardened my heart to him. And I think he knew that. Martin Luther King, Jr. said, "Darkness cannot drive out darkness; only light can do that. Hate cannot drive out hate; only love can do that." My love for Dad, which was unreturned for so long, had begun to soften his heart, driving out darkness and hate.

Janie's Dad

A glimmer of light also shown in one other corner of darkness that year.

When I'd experienced that ugly incident at my friend

Janie's house, I didn't tell my parents about it because I knew they would *go off*. But I'd shared it with some of my boys who were really angry on my behalf. They were mad that, although Mr. Henderson had no respect for me, I'd respected his home and his freedom to be who he was in his home. Honestly, it had been a hard position to be in as a teenager! I'd always been taught to take the high road, but that's much easier said than done. At the time, I'd tried to just shake it off and move on.

After one of our winning home games at Liberty, I was leaving the locker room when a man approached me. He was white and about my dad's age. As he got closer, I recognized him as Janie's dad. I hadn't seen him since that fateful dinner years before.

What on earth? What is he doing here?

Having no idea what he would say or do, I felt safer knowing that there were still fans in the stands and other guys leaving the locker room.

He approached me sheepishly and asked, "Rashad, do you have a minute?

"Sure," I answered, curious.

"Rashad, I want to apologize to you."

What?

He continued, "I'm sorry for what happened so long ago. I have a lot of respect for you."

Because I'd lost touch with Janie, I didn't know how Mr. Henderson knew anything about me anymore. Maybe he read that I was playing ball at Liberty.

"Thank you, sir," I answered, "I appreciate that."

I reached out to shake his hand, and he took my hand in his.

Before we parted ways, Mr. Henderson added again, "I have a lot of respect for you."

I was in shock! What on earth had happened in that man's life that had caused his heart to change so drastically?

If I hadn't come home to be with Dad, that moment might never have happened. I was seeing the positive results from a difficult decision I'd made as a kid. A decision a lot of people thought was crazy. But I'd known then—and I know now—that I'd done the right thing by refusing to fight hate with hate.

NFL Combine

While my future may have looked different if I'd stayed at Pitt, I never regretted going home. I got to see change in my family, in my community, and even in my opportunities as an athlete.

During my senior year, I was invited to participate in four different collegiate all-star games. Those invitations, to games where I would be viewed by NFL scouts, felt as though God had honored my decision to return to Virginia to be with my family. Yes, my choice had been a risk. But despite not playing for a Division I school, I was still being given the opportunity to be considered to play at the next level.

The North vs. South game, also known as the Senior

Bowl, was held at the University of South Alabama, in Mobile. It's where I'd finally have the chance to prove myself. Butch and Bryan prepped me by offering insight into the mindset of NFL scouts. They told me that these scouts would be asking themselves, "Did Rashad leave Pitt because he couldn't handle the competition?" Knowing that they might assume that was the case, I vowed to prove them wrong.

Coaching staff members from the NFL teams with the worst records of the season were given the opportunity to coach at the Senior Bowl. These were the same teams that would also be given first pick in the NFL draft. That year I was coached by staff from the Jacksonville Jaguars. As the NFL team that had been second from the bottom that year, I knew the Jaguars would have the second-round pick in the NFL draft. In addition to seeing me play, these coaches got to know me personally, and they saw the work ethic I brought to practice every day.

I killed it in that game. Finishing with the most rushing yards, I was named MVP. Grateful for the recognition, I breathed a prayer to God, asking that it would be enough to earn me a spot in the league.

After the Senior Bowl, I enjoyed my last three months of school. Toward the end of that final year of college, I was hanging out with Dad one Sunday evening after a great day of eating and playing spades with family and friends. Because the NFL draft was one week away, and graduation was three weeks away, we all had a lot to talk about. Everyone offered their opinions about what team they wanted to draft me.

While it was fun to play around and guess, the truth was that I would have been thrilled to have been drafted by any team in the league.

After everyone else had gone home and Mom was puttering around, cleaning up in the kitchen, Dad and I sat down to watch reruns of *Sanford and Son*. We hadn't spoken much, but that was okay.

I was sitting in a comfy armchair and Dad was stretched out on the couch. Rolling over to look me in the eye, he said, in his matter of fact way, "It don't matter if you make it or not. I'm proud of you."

I really can't describe the reaction those words ignited in my heart. Although I was twenty-three, I felt like a little boy again. And that little boy, who'd been waiting to hear those words his whole life, pretty much melted.

"Thanks, Dad," I answered. "That means a lot."

As he returned to watching our show, I continued to hold those words that would be etched in my heart forever.

Sometimes people say that when you've waited for something a long time, it's never as good as you imagined it would be. That wasn't true for me that night. The words I longed to hear from my dad felt just as good as I always hoped and imagined they would.

The Draft

A week later, my family prepared to watch the second day of the NFL draft together.

The two-day event includes seven rounds of picks. The reason the team with the poorest record the previous season picks first, and the team that had the best season picks last, is because the draft was designed to create a league in which teams are matched as evenly as possible. Each team has the opportunity to pick or trade a player in each round.

The draft was held in New York that year and telecast on ESPN. I had watched the first day of the draft, when the first-round picks were chosen, with my college roommates Mamadou Baldé, Corey Rasberry, and Doncel Bolt. On the second day of the draft, my family and friends gathered with me at a church Butch was affiliated with, Mosaic Church, to watch the second through seventh rounds on ESPN.

That might have been the most nervous I've ever felt.

Imagine yourself at recess, lined up with all the other kids, waiting to be picked for a team. Team captains who you desperately hope will choose you walk past the row of hopefuls, surveying you along with the others, and—pick after pick after pick—they choose someone *other* than you. One by one, you watch your friends get selected while you remain in the line, wondering what you might have done to make yourself a more attractive player. Now imagine yourself in that scene with a captive audience of your closest 20 or 30 loved ones. The only reason they are there is to watch and wait anxiously for you to be picked. The hard reality of this situation is that lots of people won't be picked, and you might be among them.

Wanting to create a fun, chill atmosphere, Butch had set

up pool and ping pong tables for folks who came to support me, to have some fun. We projected ESPN on a big screen. It was broadcast during primetime, which meant 8 p.m. on the East Coast. Mom brought food, and the room looked and felt like a party.

When I wasn't selected in the second round, we all agreed that it wasn't a big deal. There were still five rounds left. With 32 teams choosing, that meant 160 more picks. Most of those teams wanted to keep about three to five running backs on a 53-player roster. I knew there were a number of running back spots to be filled, so there'd be more chosen than the typical eight to ten percent. But as the rounds went on, and we watched other running backs get selected—some whom we had never even heard of—it grew harder and harder to stay in good spirits. My phone was ringing off the hook, and each time it rang I'd pick up and tell my friends, who were also watching ESPN, to stop calling me! I didn't want my phone to ring at all unless it was an NFL team.

In the bottom left corner of the television screen was a ticker feed of NFL analyst Mel Kiper's favorite picks. In rounds one through three, Mel's #1 best picks were chosen during the round in which they first appeared. And then for four straight rounds, beginning with round four, his list pegged me as the #1 best pick. But I wasn't picked in round four, five, or even six.

I couldn't understand how that could be possible. I felt a heavy mix of disappointment, sadness, and embarrassment pooling in my gut. Before the start of the seventh round, 21 other running backs had been selected, and I wasn't one of them. The mood in the room, which had been so buoyant a few hours earlier, had mellowed to a pretty dismal level.

As the ESPN commentator began to announce, "This pick just in . . .", my phone rang. I could see it wasn't one of my goofy, overly excited friends, because it was from a blocked number. I clicked to pick up.

"Is this Rashad Jennings?" asked a man's voice on the other end.

"Yes, sir," I answered, stunned.

He continued, "This is the personal assistant for Coach Jack Del Rio of the Jacksonville Jaguars."

I remembered Coach Del Rio from the Senior Bowl at Mobile.

Eager, I answered, "Hey, man, how you doing?"

Eyeballing the ticker tape along the bottom of the screen as I spoke, I read that I was selected by the Jaguars. Although I still had a reading comprehension deficit, I tell you what—I was able to focus enough to read that sentence! My family and friends erupted into cheers and applause that made it hard to hear on the phone. Even though I was talking with a Jaguar coach, I still felt dumbfounded by the announcement. It was a lot to process.

Before I could answer with an enthusiastic, "Yes," my phone lost service and dropped the call! I scrambled to step outside the building, hoping to call him back from a spot with better reception. But because he'd called from a blocked number, I had no way to call him back. I feared Jacksonville might accept my hang up as a no and make another pick! Feeling like I might have just blown the biggest opportunity of my life, all I could do was wait helplessly outside—while trying to signal my happy family not to follow me—and hope he'd call back.

A wait that lasted less than a minute felt like hours. When Jacksonville dialed me back, I apologized profusely.

Thankfully, he was still in good spirits and reiterated, "Rashad, we want you to be a Jacksonville Jaguar."

He went on to explain that they'd arrange a flight for me to go to Jacksonville, and they'd overnight a playbook to my house.

"Congratulations," he said. "You made it! Get ready for the NFL!"

When I stepped back inside, my family hugged me and we all jumped up and down. Three years earlier, when I'd chosen to transfer from a successful Division I school to a virtually unknown Division 1-AA school, this moment had been unthinkable. At that time, an ESPN announcer had predicted that I was throwing away my NFL dream. And though I was committed to honoring my family, part of me had feared he was right.

But Butch, who was in the room that night and almost suffocated me with his congratulatory hug, had never lost sight of the dream that we both knew was bigger than me. It had been eight years since the Lord had spoken through that pastor visiting Butch's church in Raleigh. And over the course of those eight years, there were a lot of moments when it would have been easy to doubt the vision would become a reality. In ninth grade, I was a heavy kid with asthma. The next year I dropped out of football altogether. The following year the coach didn't play me until he was forced to in the last game of the season. After 12th grade, my transcript wasn't processed by the NCAA clearinghouse in time to begin Pitt in the fall. And although my strong season at Pitt made it seem like I might have what it took to make it to the NFL, that future changed when I transferred to Liberty to support my family.

During those stress-filled hours we'd spent hearing the names of 21 other running backs selected before me, the promise seemed as far away as it had ever been. I was the last running back chosen in the 2009 NFL draft.

Honestly, I believe I understood how the Israelites felt wandering around in the desert. God had clearly selected them as his #1 pick, but it must have felt like they'd been tricked or lost their connection—not for sixty seconds, but for forty years! And like me, I'm sure they were asking themselves, "Wait, we were supposed to be favored, right? Did we misunderstand? Does God really have our back? Does God even care about us?" But as it was with Israel, it was with me—God seems to have a special place in his heart for underdogs.

If that's you, I want you to know that God's got you. No matter where you're headed—whether you've locked your eye on the prize like I did or you can't figure out what classes to take next year—God has good for you. And to experience that good, God asks you to be faithful right where you are.

If you're in a small school or community that doesn't offer all the honors or advanced placement classes that larger schools might, do what you can to flourish and excel in the classes available to you. If your family can't afford to send you to elite sports or music camps, give 110 percent and put in the practice to become the best you can be. If you're working a job or caring for younger siblings and can't get lots of extracurriculars on your college applications, work hard at your job and show love to your family.

When you're not yet where you want to be, your job is to do what you can where you are. There are a million small and big choices you can make to achieve that, but *if* you are faithful to what God has put before you, you'll end up right where you're supposed to be.

CHAPTER 12

GOING PRO

Training camp in Jacksonville was, as I once said to my pastor: h-e-double-hockey-sticks.

For an entire month, we had two rigorous practices every day, from eight in the morning until ten at night. At the end of that month, just 53 of the 100 guys at camp would make the team. Each one of us had to bring our "A" game every day.

In addition to the grueling workouts, the hazing of rookies—now banned in the NFL—was brutal. Rookies were routinely thrown into the cold tub—a bathtub-sized vat of ice water—which was painfully freezing. And any resistance only guaranteed a worse fate. Rookies were also given crazy haircuts: picture a circle being shaved into the top of your head, or the left half of your hair being shaved off. Some guys even had their eyebrows shaved off while they slept! It was during my rookie year when I realized the importance of eyebrows. Some of the players who had been doing great at camp began to struggle because, without eyebrows, their sweat would run right into their eyes, making them unable to see on the field.

I'd been prepared for the physical challenges of training, but I hadn't considered the social ones. My one-bedroom apartment was the first place I'd ever lived on my own. Until that point, I'd been all about family and team. It was weird to return home in the evenings and find everything exactly as I'd left it.

Almost.

The previous owner of my apartment had left a fruit basket for me that remained untouched on the dining room table for weeks. Eventually fruit flies began to breed there, and those little guys became my friends. When I came home each night, I'd hit the basket, send them into orbit, and check on them. They were my boys! (So, yeah, I was a little lonely.) One day after practice, my teammate Don Carey came over. I told him to make himself at home. He went to grab a piece of fruit and got the shock of his life when my roommates began to swarm.

I laughed as I said, "So, you met my boys, huh?"

And he replied, "Man, you need a girlfriend!"

Making Money

Adjusting to practices, hazing, and loneliness were the hard parts. What was not so difficult was getting paid! Although I'd signed my contract, and understood that I'd be getting paid well, receiving my first paycheck made it *real*. Although I wasn't earning the kind of salary that would be broadcast on ESPN, that first check was *much* more money than I'd ever had in my pocket before. Instead of leaving it in my pocket, though, I put it right in the bank.

NFL players are notorious for blowing through cash. Because the average career span for a running back in the NFL is about two seasons, I knew it was important to be smart about each of those paychecks. But not every guy on my team saw it the same way.

Other rookies were purchasing cars and houses, and wanted to know what I was buying. They'd ask, "What'd you get, Rashad?"

"Nothing," I answered.

It was true. In fact, the guys liked to make fun of me for it.

Even though I could afford to buy new ones, I kept wearing the same clothes I owned. (I figure if you brush your teeth and have a nice haircut, you can make anything look good!) And unlike most of my teammates, I was still driving the same car I had in high school! It was a gray 2000 Chevy Impala and it got me where I needed to go. I thought it was a really smooth car, so I said I was going to drive it until the wheels fell off.

A few weeks after training camp ended, my girlfriend flew into town for the weekend. (I *did* have a girlfriend— she just lived out of state.) I knew that if I left my apartment complex when her plane landed, we'd end up at the baggage carousel about the same time. So when she texted, "Hey, I landed," I hustled down to the parking garage and hopped in my car to pick her up.

I was heading north on Interstate 95 when I felt a major shift in my car. Turning down my music, I noticed the car tilting to the left. A second later, I heard and felt the bottom of the car scraping the pavement. After pulling over to the shoulder, I got out and eyeballed the length of the driver's side of my car. *Dang! My wheel had literally fallen off!* Can you imagine driving down the road and seeing your car's wheel rolling down the street? That's what happened to me.

I chased down the wheel, hauled it back, pulled the spare out of the trunk, put it on, and headed to the airport. Long story short—I didn't get to the baggage carousel when she did. While I thought it was kind of funny, as well as an understandable reason to have been late to the airport, my girlfriend didn't quite agree.

Maybe it *was* time for a new car. After all, I did vow to drive it until the wheels fell off, never expecting that it would actually happen.

I kept the Impala around for a while longer, but luckily, there was a car out there just waiting for me. Eugene Monroe was our team's first-round draft pick and he'd bought a 2010 black-on-black Camaro with suede interior. He'd put in a sound system you could hear a mile away. He'd added all the bells and whistles, and had even souped-up the engine!

It was my good fortune that, as an offensive tackle, Eugene was a huge guy and therefore wasn't very comfortable in the Camaro. I said to myself, *He's going to get tired of that car one day. Just wait.* And, as I'd predicted, about a year and a half later, I approached him and offered to buy it. Eugene was a nice guy—and I was a pretty good negotiator—so I got that car for pennies on the dollar, and I still own it today.

The First Big Purchase

Because I knew I wanted to last much longer than the standard two or three years most running backs played in the league, I started asking veteran players what steps they took to take care of their bodies. The Jaguar's starting running back, Maurice Jones-Drew, told me that he took a specific regimen of vitamins. When I asked who prescribed them, he introduced me to Dr. Julie Buckley. Dr. Buckley treats patients holistically, which means she uses a variety of methods to promote health. Dr. Buckley not only prescribed vitamins that best met my body's needs, she also became like my mom-away-from-home, inviting me to dinner every Saturday night. Julie and her family were much better company than the fruit flies!

For those nights when I wasn't eating at Julie's house, I decided to invest in a chef who'd prepare healthy whole foods for me. Whole foods are foods that are as close as possible to their natural state, without all the chemicals and processing. My fast food days were long behind me. I wanted to be fueling my body with the healthiest, most efficient foods possible, so hiring a chef was one more way I was investing in my longevity as a player.

While I was still driving around in that car that had lost a wheel on the freeway, I made my first significant purchase when I bought—wait for it—a hyperbaric oxygen chamber. Doctors often suggest an oxygen chamber to patients with wounds that aren't healing. An oxygen chamber increases the amount of oxygen the blood can carry, promoting health and healing. For a person who's overall healthy, especially a professional athlete, the chamber facilitates the body's healing from the daily wear and tear of practice and games. I still wasn't interested in impressing people with fly clothes or a shiny new ride, and I didn't yet know anything about the stock market. So I figured I would invest in something I did know about and could control—*myself.* If it worked like I'd been told it would, I would be investing in my career by adding to my performance and prolonging my years as a professional athlete. So a hyperbaric chamber was my first big purchase and, yes, it was about the price of a new car. I've never regretted it.

I chose a portable hyperbaric chamber so that I could travel with it when we were on the road. It was nine feet long and five feet wide. I still have it to this day. Constructed like a tent, the chamber blows up like a big bubble when turned on. Inside, the air pressure increases to three times the normal pressure, allowing human lungs to take in more oxygen, which is then carried throughout the body via the blood. This treatment increases the body's ability to fight infection and to heal injured tissue. The very first time I was inside the chamber, I felt the difference in my body. Although the other rookies had to share rooms at training camp and on the road, I had my own room because the chamber made a lot of external noise. But inside this magic machine, I slept like a baby.

Investing in People

Besides investing in making my body stronger and more efficient, I also wanted to invest in people. It would be a few years before I'd launch the Rashad Jennings Foundation, but since I was serious about helping people, I started at home. I knew my parents had been struggling with debt, and I wanted to help.

After my second year as a Jaguar, I sat my family down— the way they'd always been calling *me* to family meetings—to discuss how we'd work together to get my parents out of the $50,000 debt they'd accrued. After crunching the numbers, I realized it would be a long time before my parents could dig themselves out of that hole. And while I finally did have the resources to help, I wanted my parents to have the personal satisfaction of knowing they paid down their debt. At our meeting, in order to calculate what they could afford, I asked my parents to tell me how much money they were bringing in each month. Based on that number, I figured out a realistic loan repayment plan. But instead of paying that money to the bank, at 12% interest, they could pay it to me. After the meeting, I went to the bank, paid off their loan, and then extended a loan to them from the "bank of Rashad Jennings", a loan they could pay back monthly, without the burden of interest.

An NFL player representative heard about this approach, and shared it with other players so they could help their own families do the same thing.

I am grateful to God that I've been blessed with the resources I need, and I count it as a privilege to use some of those resources to help others. But I didn't just want to make a difference with dollars. In addition to investing my money, I also wanted to devote time to helping others. Although I didn't have a lot of extra time due to my training schedule, I set aside two hours every Tuesday for community outreach, most often seeking opportunities that allowed me to motivate kids.

One day I was speaking to a class of middle schoolers, knowing that their teacher, Mrs. Springer, had assigned them a research paper in which they had to write about professional athletes. As I was telling them about a day in the life of a pro athlete, they were scribbling down everything I was saying.

A week later, when those seventh graders turned in their papers, they'd all cited Jacksonville Jaguars running back *Rashad Jennings.*

When Mrs. Springer reported that she'd received some great papers, I thought of my tenth grade English teacher, Miss Hudson, who gave me an F+ when I cited "The Mind of Rashad Jennings" in my paper about Dr. Martin Luther King, Jr.

I asked Mrs. Springer for copies of the papers that had earned As, and packed them in my suitcase before flying home the following weekend.

Just before school let out on Friday, I parked in the faculty lot of Jefferson Forest High School. I walked into the school as students were flooding out the doors at dismissal. Winding my way through football players and cheerleaders, band members and mathletes, I found Miss Hudson's old room on the second floor.

Miss Hudson was erasing the white board when I entered the room.

As she turned around, I slapped 11 stapled research papers onto her desk and said, "Check this out!"

Curious, she picked up the first paper and began to read it. A big smile broke out across her face as she skimmed each one, glancing down at the students' footnotes.

"Rashad," she said, "I always knew you were going to achieve whatever you put your mind to. There was no doubt in my mind! I knew you were going to be successful."

Her affirmation meant a lot to me. I was finally a credible source.

If You Want to Make a Difference

Choosing how we use the resources we've been given—our health, our relationships, our finances—is one of those *ifs* in life. And the way we navigate the *if* determines the outcome we achieve.

For example, when I was a kid, I spotted a fully-equipped truck and told my mom I wanted one. She promised me that *if* I worked hard, I'd be able to buy one someday. But the beginning of my rookie season was not that day. Rather than blowing my money on stuff I wanted, I chose to live within my means and put the money I was earning into my career, investments, savings, family, and causes I believed in. Those habits didn't begin when I signed with the Jaguars. They started when I was in high school and college; even then I tried to be careful with the ways I spent my money and used my time. (Except for video games . . . *Halo 3* was my weakness!)

If you want to make an impact with your life by becoming all that you can be and blessing those around you, now is the time to start. You may not have a major league sports contract, but you might have an allowance or a part-time job. You may not have lots of extra time to volunteer, but you could make wiser use of some of the hours you spend on social media. The choices you're making today are shaping who you'll be in the future.

Make the most of them!

CHAPTER 13

THE UPS AND DOWNS

When I was little, I looked at the guys playing in the NFL with awe. Like any kid, I was a bit blinded by my vision of what wearing an NFL jersey would be like. Even though I had two older brothers who'd played in the league, and who knew the ups and downs, I was too young to care about the downs. (I don't mean touchdowns! That's the only thing I did care about.) When I imagined a future as a player, I saw only the glory of sprinting down the field and flying into the end zone. From the comfort of our living room, the NFL looked like a dream life to me.

The reality, I was learning, was a bit different.

The Work

For starters, there wasn't a day that I wasn't working to take care of my body.

Once a week I received chiropractic care. It was required maintenance after running so many miles—kind of like getting an oil change for your car.

Twice a week I received Muscle Activation Therapy, which targets the attachment of the muscle to the bone. This is a fascinating process. For example, when my shoulder would seize up, a therapist worked my left pec, my right hip, and my left pinky toe to release the tension in my shoulder! Crazy, right? But it worked.

Twice a week I'd also get a massage, which focused more on the belly of the muscle in order to flush the lactic acid out of my system.

And, of course, I continued to work out like a mad man. On each NFL team, one trainer is expected to get 53 very different men ready to perform. The result of that uneven ratio is that no one receives training tailored to their own body and abilities, so no one is working at full capacity. While I appreciated what these trainers offered us, I wasn't about to let someone else dictate my training regimen. That didn't mean that I was going to slack off in practice. No, I'd give 100 percent. But I wouldn't stop there.

Each day, when our team's conditioning was complete, I'd continue with my own regimen, just like I had in high school and college. On any given day that might mean sled work, ladder drills, interval sprints on an elliptical, or pool work. The training pool was about eight feet wide by 12 feet long, and there was a treadmill on the bottom. When the jets were turned on, they'd blast right at me to provide resistance as I ran on the treadmill. I'd have to fight to stand up, let alone run! It's a great workout that reduces the impact on your joints because there's no ground resistance.

Less Control

I was happy to put in long hours of training to improve my skills and endurance, but there were some factors that I couldn't control. As it is for every player, one of those was playing time. When I was drafted to Jacksonville, I knew I'd be sitting because the Jaguar's starting running back was Maurice Jones-Drew. In my opinion, this guy deserves to be in the Hall of Fame! A year earlier, when we lived together while training for the combine in Florida, I was honored to be staying with such a talented baller. I counted it a privilege to train with Maurice, never expecting to be on the same team as him. So when Jacksonville drafted me, I was excited for the opportunity to learn from him—even if that meant learning from the bench.

In addition to the amount of playing time I was given, I also couldn't control injuries. A shoulder injury my first year as a Jaguar meant I had to sit out four games. My second year I missed one game due to a concussion. My third year, I expected to be a starter but in a preseason exhibition game I suffered a grade 1 MCL sprain. Instead of the prescribed four to six weeks off, the team put me on the injured reserve list, which meant I missed the entire season! Because I knew the care I gave my body—from eating right to sleeping in the chamber—this was a really hard pill to swallow. And sure enough, I was back to full speed in just two and a half weeks. But because I was on "injured reserve," I still sat.

All right, I reasoned, *I'm going to keep studying my game and stay in shape.* I also got more deeply involved with volunteering in the community, and I took a cooking class from my personal chef so I could begin cooking for myself.

The fourth year was rough too, and when my four-year contract ended, I wasn't signed again by the Jaguars.

Unable to control whether or not I'd be signed by another team, I went home to wrap my head around what I'd do next. After spending some time in Virginia with my folks, I decided to return to Florida to train and to ask God if my time in the league was done. At that time, I was in the zone. My workouts were as strong as ever, I was eating great food, and still doing Muscle Activation Therapy to maximize the function of my muscles.

Early one morning, I received a call from a number I didn't recognize. On the other end was a coach from the Oakland Raiders, inviting me to do a workout with them. This was my chance to show them what I could do, and I knew I was ready for it.

After the call, I continued with my daily routine and headed to the gym around nine. About an hour later, I was under the squat bar when the weights on the left side, which weren't properly secured, slid off the bar. The sudden shift of weight—about 115 pounds—hitting the ground forced my body to compensate for the imbalance, tweaking something in my lower back.

Seriously? This had to happen *the day* the Raiders called? They wanted me to fly to California the next day, and to be ready to work out that week.

Considering that sitting, standing, and walking were all uncomfortable, I knew there was no way I could sprint at full speed. I spent the day doing everything I could to alleviate the pain. I got two hours of massage, went in to see my chiropractor, and was even able to book an appointment with an acupuncturist, but nothing helped. Feeling desperate, I went home, iced my back, and headed to bed, hoping rest would make me feel better.

The next morning, my back was still locked up. Unable to lift myself out of bed, I rolled onto the floor and used my legs to stand. I had no idea how I'd even make it through the morning, let alone a workout the following day, but I forced myself to pack and get to the airport. Sitting in my seat during takeoff was excruciating, so I stood for the rest of the flight.

The stakes were as high as they'd ever been. I knew that my performance the next day wouldn't just affect Oakland's opinion of me. If their staff saw me hurting, word would spread, and I wouldn't be getting calls from any team.

I showed up to train with the Raiders at seven the next morning with a big smile on my face! This was a crucial moment for my career, and I was determined not to blow it. Throughout the day I figured out ways to move through drills, sprints, and patterns without cutting right, which was the most painful movement. During one of the most difficult days of my career, I continued to smile and perform.

In the NFL, coaches move around the league just like players do, and one of the Raiders coaches had been our quarterback coach in Jacksonville. I knew he could vouch for my skill, character, and work ethic. At the end of the day, as I packed up my gym bag, he came over to speak to me.

"Shad, we want to sign you!" he announced with delight.

The effort had been worth it! I'd made the team.

Wanting to seal the announcement with an embrace, he reached out to grab me in a big bear hug. I wanted to duck away, but I knew I had to receive his celebratory hug.

"Rashad," he exclaimed, "we can't wait to get you out here."

With pain shooting through my back, I raised my eyebrows and smiled, saying, "Yeah, can't wait!"

As I left the field and headed back to my hotel, I kept up the façade that I wasn't in excruciating pain. It was a rough night, and it wasn't until I got on the plane the next morning that I breathed a deep sigh of relief, and thought, *I made it.*

Facing Obstacles

A lot of what I believed the life of a pro football player to be when I was a kid was true. I won't lie—scoring a touchdown is one of the best feelings on earth! But, as with anything we tackle in life, the job also had its challenges and frustrations. I couldn't eat and drink whatever I felt like. I had to put long hours into training and caring for my body. I couldn't determine what other people thought of me. I didn't decide how much playing time I got. I suffered injuries. Every day I was making decisions that would determine *if* I'd become the person God had designed me to be.

"If I eat this Big Mac . . ."

"If I settle for the workout assigned to me . . ."

"If I let others define who I am supposed to be . . ."

"If I cop an attitude about not playing today . . ."

"If I allow this injury to determine my future . . ."

The way I answered every one of those *ifs* would, and did, determine my success.

The same is true for you. The small decisions you make *this week* are the ones that are shaping the course of your life. Never is that truer than when you encounter obstacles. Did you bomb the SAT? You're the person who decides *if* you'll buckle down, study, and take it again. Did you fail to perform well on the court or playing field? You're the one who decides *if* you'll put in the effort required to succeed next time. Did the person you want to date turn you down? You decide *if* you'll interpret one "no" as a judgment about who you are, or *if* you'll give yourself space to heal and move on. And maybe you've had to face an obstacle in your life that's a lot bigger than academics, sports, or dating. No matter what challenges you've encountered, you have the choice to face and overcome them. *If* you decide to.

Being a Raider

Thankfully, with a bit more time, and the help of my oxygen chamber, my back healed. When I joined the Raiders I was able to give them my all. My first year with the team, I won offensive player of the year and team MVP, two reasons why I didn't expect my first year to be my *only* year with them.

As the season was winding down, I spoke to the head coach, the owner, and the general manager, who all promised I'd continue to be a Raider. They even offered to match any other deal I received.

"Relax," they reassured me. "And stay in shape."

Cool. I could do that.

Because I hadn't signed a new contract with the Raiders, and because I'd completed five seasons, I was technically an unrestricted free agent when my one-year contract expired at the end of the season. March 11 was option day for free agency, which happens when a team releases a player making him available to possibly sign with another team. The very first hour teams could begin contacting players, I received a call from the New York Giants offering me a deal.

Of all the teams in the league, I understood why the Giants called. It was the same reason I had heard from the Raiders a year earlier—they'd seen me play. During this season, I'd killed it when the Raiders played the Giants and they remembered that.

Flattered to have been noticed, I politely listened to the terms, assuming I'd still be playing for the Raiders. Thanking them for the offer, and letting them know I'd get back to them, I hung up, feeling more than a little pleased with the interest.

My next call was to the money man at the Raiders who negotiates contracts. When it comes to finalizing the deal, it's this guy—not the coach, owner, or the general manager. When I gave him the terms of the Giants' offer, he balked.

"We can't do that," he announced.

I calmly relayed the previous conversations I'd had that made me confident the Raiders would match the Giants' offer. He wasn't budging. I really wanted to stay with the Raiders, but he was making it clear that they wouldn't increase my salary to match the Giants'.

I wish I could say that it all came down to numbers. But it didn't. Our difficult conversation communicated to me that I wasn't valued in Oakland the same way I would be elsewhere. It made me more willing to entertain the possibility of playing for New York. When I called them back to discuss bumping the salary a bit higher, their answer was, "Yeah, no problem." And that's where numbers *did* come in to the picture. If Oakland wasn't willing to match the first offer, they certainly weren't going to match the second one.

I didn't want my decision to be all about money, and it wasn't. To be signed to a team that believed in what I could accomplish, after five years in the league, wasn't something I took lightly. I didn't want to leave my teammates in Oakland, and the decision wasn't an easy one. But I knew then, and know now, it was the right one for me.

When you're faced with making a decision that will impact your future—whether it's what college to attend, what job to take, or who you'll share your life with—it's important to identify the pros and the cons. Weighing what you'll gain and lose helps you make the best decision. And sometimes the best decision, which might not be obvious to everyone, will put you in a place where you're surrounded by people who will make you better in the long run. The key is resisting the urge to make the choices others want you to make—like staying at Pitt would have been for me—but rather, making decisions based on your own values and commitments.

A week after I spoke to the Giants, I was waiting for a plane to New York City's LaGuardia airport. After boarding the plane and stowing my bag, I sat down and tweeted, "I'm on my way to be a Giant."

CHAPTER 14

FINALLY CONNECTING

Several years before I was born, in the late 1970s, the weekly intro to *ABC's Wide World of Sports* featured iconic sporting moments, the beautiful and the brutal, that the announcer billed as "the thrill of victory and the agony of defeat." That kind of describes my first two games for the Giants.

In our first regular season game, against the Cardinals— my favorite team as a boy—we were gunning to tie the score when I caught a short pass from Eli Manning at the fifteen-yard line. I know this sounds like it's going to be the "thrill of victory", but unfortunately, I slipped and fumbled. I felt like I was standing before a captive audience with no clothes on! Literally no one had touched me because no one had been anywhere near me. We ended up losing by 11 points. When the media barraged me after the game, I admitted my mistake and assured them that we'd be ready for the following week's game against the Texans.

The next week, against Houston, I rushed for 176 yards, the team's highest yardage total in two years. That was definitely the "thrill" part! And I'd go on to experience many more of those disappointing lows and exhilarating highs, unwanted injuries and exuberant end zone dances over the three years I played for the Giants.

There was one important fan who hadn't seen me play for the Giants in MetLife stadium yet, and that was my dad. When Butch and Bryan had played in the NFL, Dad had been healthy enough to attend some of their games. But because of his amputation and other recent health complications, Dad had only attended one of my pro games. With a lot of effort, Mom and my brothers had gotten him to Jacksonville a few years earlier. What cracked us up was that although he might have had a bit of awareness of what was happening on the field, his real attention was with the cheerleaders. (Butch and Bryan can attest to this!)

Thankfully, that didn't end up being the only game he watched—or didn't watch. A series of events that would eventually land him in the stands again, began at one of the Giants' team dinners.

Typically, Saturday was a travel day, but when the Giants were playing at home, we'd meet in a hotel on Saturday for meetings, meals, and chapel for those who wanted it. Chapel was optional, but for those who opted out of the team, there was a $15,000 motivational fine!

The dinnertime meal was catered, and we'd all break off to eat at round tables. Sometimes there would be a college football game playing. And most of the guys had caught on that if they sat at my table, there would always be an interesting topic for discussion.

At one of those dinners, I wanted us to discuss the question, "Why do you play?" I set it up by reminding my teammates that there were about 1,600 people *in the universe* who got to do what we do. In my mind, that makes playing professional football quite a privilege. One by one, guys shared their reasons for playing football.

When it was my turn, I shared a bit about my rocky relationship with my dad. Despite our difficult beginnings, I'd seen his heart soften toward me over the years. And as I felt myself get a little emotional, I was reminded that my own heart had been softened as well.

At the end of the meal, I encouraged the guys to hold the *reason* for playing ball in their hearts the next day. And I quietly vowed that when we took the field against the Texans on Sunday, I'd be playing that game for Dad.

Good Luck

There were actually a lot of reasons I played football every week. I played because it had opened the door for me to earn a college degree. I played because it had been my childhood dream. And I played because the platform it afforded me gave me a way to give back to others. That next day, as I prepared myself for the game against Texas, I reminded myself that this was going to be an especially big game for me—I was playing for Dad. I was going to do something special for him. Since the amputation of his leg, he'd also suffered a stroke. On that day, I'd be his legs.

Before I left for the stadium, I got a call from my family, wishing me good luck in the game. After I spoke to Mom, I asked her to put Dad on the line.

"Dad," I explained, "I'm gonna be playing this game with you in my heart and mind. This game is dedicated to you."

"Aw, thanks, Shad," he replied politely.

"I mean it, Dad," I continued. "Every down, you're going to be on my mind!"

My dad, who'd once seemed so fierce to me, sort of giggled at that.

And then, with his stroke-impaired speech, he said, "Go kick butt!"

As I hung up the phone, I was still laughing about that one.

A few hours later, after we'd suited up and warmed up, I had the chance to lead a prayer for the guys who wanted to join in. That day, it turned out to be about 45 of the 60 guys on our team. We circled up and held hands, and before I prayed I shared part of the conversation we'd had at dinner the previous night.

"Today," I instructed, "I want everyone to have someone in mind that you're playing for. My dad doesn't have healthy legs, and I do. So I'm going to be running for him."

And that's what I did. Minute by minute, down by down,

quarter by quarter, I held my dad in my heart as I played. By the end of the game, I'd achieved a career high in rushing, as well as most yards in a game, making me the leading rusher in the NFL. While telecasting the game, ESPN had taken notice of my success on the field. When Josina Anderson interviewed me after the game, I wasn't shy about sharing the reason the game had been so fruitful.

"What makes this game special," I said, "was that I played with my dad in mind."

I also explained about his limitations, and how I wanted to use my body to honor him.

When I left the stadium, I called Dad.

Picking up the phone, he said, without hesitation, "Rashad, I'm so proud of you."

You know I didn't hear those words often from him. But they meant the world to me on those rare occasions I did.

My success on the field that day correlated directly to the *reason* I was playing. Just as it had been when I left Pitt to support my parents, I was driven by a very specific answer to the question, "Why?"

When you set your mind to do something that matters— whether it's taking a stand against injustice, giving back to those in need, sacrificing for a family member, or launching an important initiative—you have to cling to the *why* that propelled you into action in the first place. When the going gets rough, which it will, that *why* will be the fuel that energizes you to stick with it. Know your *why* and let it move you.

A Possibility

The snippet of our interview where I mentioned my dad had sparked an idea in Josina's mind. Wanting to follow up and learn more about my family, she visited my folks in Lynchburg, to interview them. During that interview, she asked Dad, "What would it mean for you to see Rashad play in the stadium as a Giant?"

He listened to her question, and the moment the words were out of her mouth, he burst into tears.

"It would be a dream come true," he said, in a broken voice. "I'd love to see him play again."

After the interview, as Mom helped Dad wipe the tears off his face, Josina quietly spoke to me about the possibility.

"We can put him up in the press box," Josina offered. "If he's able, we'll make it happen."

I felt giddy inside, like a little kid, at the thought of Dad being able to attend one of my games. But I was doubtful the doctors would approve it. While it was a generous offer, I couldn't let myself hold onto that hope too tightly.

Pregame

Six weeks after that interview, I was warming up before our game against the New Orleans Saints. This day was no different. I applied the same kind of intensity I'd always put into my pregame routine. In fact, *The New York Times* had featured an article and video about my elaborate routine. Writer

Bill Pennington described it in his online article in October of 2015, as "part performance art, part plyometrics and part flexibility training." He continued, "It involves dance moves, stretching and atypical agility drills that have Jennings hopping, high-stepping, skipping, bobbing, twisting and crawling—all of it mixed in with the occasional moment of quiet meditation." He wasn't wrong! And once I started that sequence, headphones strapped on, I was so focused that I noticed very little else.

. That's why I didn't notice a van driving onto the field.

The Giants running back coach at that time was Craig Johnson, who'd coached my brother Butch at Virginia Military Institute. When I was a little kid he'd playfully asked me, "Rashad, you gonna play one day?" All those years later, he was coaching me as part of the Giants' staff.

Craig was the first one to notice my family, who'd slipped out of the van and were waiting patiently on the sidelines. I was on the opposite corner of the field.

Delighted to be in on the surprise, Coach walked over with a smile on his face. "Hey, Shad, there's a kid that would love to see you."

Well, he had me there. I've always loved connecting with kids, and want to take those opportunities when I can.

"Sure," I answered, "just let me finish my warm-up."

When I'd finished my sequence, I headed across the field. Along the way I greeted players from the Saints I knew from training in the off-season. We chatted a bit, and then I finally made it across the field.

I saw a group of people and I realized that some of them had jerseys on with my number—23. The first thing I recognized was Mom's electric smile. She'd made it to a game! I was as thrilled as a kid at Christmas. Because she was Dad's primary caregiver, she hadn't been able to come to games either.

As I wrapped her in a big bear hug, I said, "Mom! Why didn't you tell me you were coming?"

And that's when I saw Dad's friend, Greg. When I'd finished hugging my mom, I walked over and shook his hand, and gave him a hug too.

Then Greg asked, "Guess who else is here?"

A few people stepped out of the way, and I saw Dad! Despite several challenging obstacles, he had showed up. For me. I kneeled to hug him, and we cried together.

Another Surgery

During my final year with the Giants, my family received more bad news. My father's left leg needed to be amputated. We were all heartbroken. While he was in rehab, my folks continued to live in Richmond, VA, rather than Lynchburg. It was the best way for Dad to get to all the appointments and therapies he needed after the amputation. When those were complete, we knew my parents would need a new living situation. Although living permanently in a nursing home was one of the options on the table for Dad, both my parents desperately wanted to move back to Lynchburg and share a home together. But their old home, the one in which I'd grown up, had very little accessible space. They'd made do there after my father's first surgery, but they really needed a better option. As my father's year of therapy drew to a close, we began to look for a home in Lynchburg that would provide the accessibility he needed.

In the meantime, Dad had to stay in a nursing home to receive the care his body needed. During that difficult period, he called me every day. He was in a lot of physical pain and struggling emotionally. We all felt so helpless during those days, made worse by the fact that we were unable to be together and support each other.

"Dad," I said one evening when we were talking, "I know how hard this is on you. I'd like to call you every night and pray with you before you go to bed. Would you like that?"

"Yes, Shad," he confirmed. I heard the emotion welling up in his voice.

From that night on, I called Dad every night around ten o'clock. I was usually at home, and I'd pause from whatever I was doing to connect with him at the end of his day.

We'd chat for a bit, and then I'd ask him, "Dad, you got anything you want us to pray for?"

Every night his response was the same, "Nah, man, just pray."

I'd pray for him, for his caregivers, and we'd pray for Mom and my brothers. And at the end of each of our calls, he'd express his affection for me.

"Love you, man," he'd say.

And every night, from the bottom of my heart, I'd echo, "I love you, too, Dad."

The Miss

Even though my dad had never been an overtly religious person, I could tell he really looked forward to our nightly prayers. They were a private exchange between us that Mom didn't even know about. When he talked to my mom one day and told her I was praying with him, she thought he'd dreamt it!

One night while out on a date, my phone rang at 11:15. I recognized the number as the nursing home where Dad was staying.

"Oh, no!" I yelped, startling my date.

Apologizing to her and briefly explaining the situation, I picked up the call.

"Man," Dad said, "did you try to call me?"

I could hear an edge of concern in his voice.

"Nah," I explained. "I wasn't home. I'm sorry, Dad!"

We took a few minutes to pray, and then he closed with the words that warmed my heart.

"Thanks," he said, sincerely. "Love you, man."

It's funny that Mom thought he was dreaming up our conversations, because each one was the stuff of my own dreams. Dad and I continued to talk and pray each night he was in the nursing home, right up until he and my mom were finally able to move into their new accessible home.

After years of longing for Dad to be at one of my games, he'd showed up for me. And in that season when he was feeling alone and forgotten, I was able to show up for him. But being a light for people doesn't always have to be praying or preaching. Often it's just a matter of showing up. Sometimes it might mean offering a listening ear. Other times you can encourage others by staying positive and holding on to hope when circumstances are hard. *If* you're willing to offer yourself—your time, your energy, and your love—to others, you can be that person who makes a difference in the lives of those around you.

CHAPTER 15

SHIFTING GEARS

One night in 2014, after leaving an autograph session at Modell's Sporting Goods store in New York, I was walking home through the city. When I say "walking," I mean I had my headphones on and was dancing around, jamming to Justin Bieber's new album, *Purpose*.

A cameraman for the entertainment and sports channel TMZ was filming in Times Square and shouted out, "Hey, Rashad! I see you're working on your dance moves! You thinking about *Dancing with the Stars*?"

Playing, I hollered back, "That would be dope!"

And while I did enjoy dancing—which any Giants' fans who saw my pregame warmup for three years could attest—I'd never had any formal dance training. Because of the leotards, remember?

Little did I know that before long, I was going to be invited to suit up for the Super Bowl—of dance.

Dancing at Last

After I was released by the Giants at the end of the 2016 season, I returned to Florida to train and stay in shape for whatever would come next. I like to pick up new hobbies during the offseason and this season, I decided on ballroom dance. I'm a big believer in the benefits of cross-training, and I was sure that even if I never made it to the New York City Ballet, the skills I learned would be great for my balance and athleticism.

The day after I signed up for dance lessons at a local studio, I got a call from *Dancing with the Stars*, inviting me to be on the show! The decision to join the show was a no-brainer for me. If I could continue to train and be available to manage the other parts of my life, I was in. The producers promised they could work around my schedule.

The first thing I did was call my mom.

"Mom," I practically shouted. "You ain't gonna believe this! I'm going to be on *Dancing with the Stars*!"

"Oh, good Lord," she sighed.

She'd learned years earlier that I was passionate about trying new things, but she was not convinced that this one had my name on it.

"Shad, you sure?" she asked hesitantly.

"Yeah, Mom. It's gonna be great!"

"Baby," she reminded me, "you wear size 14 shoes! You're gonna be stepping all over the feet of whatever poor partner you get . . ."

"Mom!" I stopped her. "I got this."

Butch and Bryan also got a kick out of the thought of me learning to dance in front of millions of viewers. They thought I'd last a few weeks. Three or four, tops.

I was determined to prove them wrong.

Preparing

I was blessed to be paired with the amazing Emma Slater. Not only would Emma be my dance partner, she'd also choreograph all our routines. For our first two weeks of rehearsal, she came to Florida where I was training. I'd begin the day with my own personal workouts, and then we'd rehearse each afternoon from one to five p.m. I knew from the first moment we met that she would not only be a fabulous coach and dance partner, but we'd also end up being friends for life.

When we moved our rehearsals to Los Angeles, where the show would be filmed, we started putting in even more hours of work each day. In a typical week, Emma would spend Monday listening to the music we'd be dancing to and she'd begin choreographing our routine. Then the two of us would get to work on Tuesday and would pretty much keep dancing until the show aired the following Monday night. It was as intense as any football training schedule I'd ever had!

We had a lot of fun together, as week after week we escaped elimination. After a series of successful dances together, we began to hope we could go all the way to the finals. In the middle of one of our rehearsals, though, I fell to the ground and cried out in pain, grabbing my ankle. Emma rushed over to check on me and evaluate my ankle. Concerned that an injury could mean the end for us, I saw the worry on her face. I also saw that she had no idea it was April first. As she checked for tenderness or swelling, I broke out in a big grin, teasing, "April Fool's!"

While the show was a lot of fun, it was also a lot of work. Emma was already a hard worker, but she told me I pushed her even further. Every week we were begging the producers to give us more time in the studio to practice. (After the season, the producers realized we had practiced for 362 hours—that was over 100 more hours than any other team in the show's history!)

As you know, I don't presume to have more natural talent or innate skill than anyone else. When I look at the successes I've been blessed with, I can only point to one thing: a strong work ethic. That's why I want to remind you that *that can be enough*. When you put your mind to something, you can achieve far more than you ever thought possible. And when you are passionate about the process, even more than the outcome, you will succeed.

If someone's told you that you can't do something— because they say you're not smart enough, fit enough, popular enough, or skilled enough—let that fuel your fire to prove them wrong!

The Love

One of the things I loved about *Dancing with the Stars* was that fans responded like they never had in the NFL. In football, the fans could love you one week and hate you and boo you the next. But on DWTS, I got so much love *every week*. Seriously, I could have tripped and fallen, and people still would have clapped and cheered. In that way, these two competitive arenas were very different from each other!

When I described to Mom how different the two experiences were, she knew why.

"Shaddy Rock," she explained, "they get to see *you*! Without the helmet! When you're out there being goofy and playing around, they finally get to see who you really are."

She wasn't wrong. Players are pretty armored up out there on the field, like rows of matching figures on a foosball table! With the exception of our signature end zone celebrations, the playing field wasn't the place to showcase unique personalities. DWTS gave me a whole new opportunity to be *me*, which was a blessing I hadn't even been expecting.

After rehearsal one evening, I was coming out of a sushi restaurant in L.A. when I finally understood how I was seen by different viewers. As I stepped out onto the sidewalk, there was a man on my left and a woman on my right. The man, who was African-American, was walking with his family and had a toddler riding on his shoulders. The woman, who was white, looked to be a few years out of high school. She was wearing a sorority sweatshirt and walking with her girl-friends. The two strangers recognized me at the same time.

The man said, "Hey, you're Rashad Jennings! From the Giants!"

And the young woman called out, "Hey, you're Rashad! From *Dancing with the Stars*!"

A quick glance at each of them suggested that these strangers probably had very little overlap in any other parts of their worlds! The three of us chatted for a bit before parting ways. While that's just a random example, building bridges like that is part of what God put me on earth to do. Whether that's in the locker room, or as an NFL Player Representative for the Giants, or between folks like those in L.A. who might not have even *seen* each other otherwise, I get a lot of satisfaction out of helping unlikely people find common ground.

Another difference between the two competitions was that not only did the DWTS fans want me to win, they could actually make it happen! I know there are some crazy-superstitious football fans out there who think that by wearing a blue ski hat on game day and eating pizza left-handed while sitting on the couch at home they can help a team win. (Hey, man, do what you've gotta do.) But with *Dancing with the Stars*, fans really did tip the scales! Each week, the judges' scores were combined with the tallies of fans who phoned in their votes. Seriously, a waitress in Lynchburg told me she voted 1,008 times! If that's not a fan, I don't know what is.

I not only wanted to do the best I could for myself, but I also wanted to show my family, who began with very little faith in #ShadTheDancer, that I could succeed at anything I put my mind to. After the first show, they were willing to entertain the possibility that I might not make a total fool of myself on national television. And several weeks later, they had a chance to see for themselves.

Most Memorable Year

The biggest night of the *Dancing with the Stars* competition for me wasn't the final dance. (Because Emma and I won Season 24, that fact may surprise a lot of people!) The dance that meant the most to me was the contemporary dance we performed the fourth week. The theme for that show was "Most Memorable Year," and it was the only week I was allowed to choose the music we'd dance to. As I thought about the most meaningful year of my life, I knew I wanted to dance to honor my dad. With such a weighty responsibility before me, I turned to my iTunes library of over 5,000 songs. Scrolling past my "soundtrack" playlist—these are the songs I want to use when I write my first movie—I opened up my "emotional" playlist of songs that make me feel deeply when I hear them. After giving it a lot of thought, I chose Katy Perry's "Unconditionally."

Although it was clearly a powerful choice in my mind, I still needed to convince Emma. When I told her I wanted to dance for my dad, she'd imagined something more upbeat.

"I love the song," she said, "but what about it moves you for your dad?"

That started a great conversation in which I was able to unpack my relationship with Dad a bit more. I still wasn't certain, though, that I had buy-in from Emma.

When I showed up at the studio bright and early Tuesday morning, I heard "Unconditionally" being piped throughout the room and saw Emma running through some moves.

"Hey!" I said, a big smile on my face. "We're doing it!"

And as Emma began to describe how she saw the dance unfold, she started crying. When *she* cried, I knew there was no way I was going to hold it together.

At the end of rehearsal that day, she warned, "Make sure you're ready, Shad."

I knew it was a tall order, but I vowed to do my best.

Showtime

The night of the show, the people I loved most in the world were seated in the audience. Although my dad would never have been able to travel by commercial airline, Jerry Falwell Jr., the Chancellor of Liberty University, offered his family's private plane so that my parents could be there. Jerry's wife, Becki, came along and brought her teenage daughter and the daughter's girlfriend. It was your basic Lynchburg to L.A. field trip. I made sure my folks stayed at Hotel Hollywood, which they totally deserved!

Because the live show went on the air at five o'clock, Emma and I were warmed up and dressed up in our dance costumes by late afternoon. We were ready to dance! It had already been a very emotional week, so my nerves were on edge as we waited backstage while the host pumped up the audience. We heard host Tom Bergeron ask, "Who do you want to win?" In the first few weeks of the show, there was just a cacophony of shouting, and you couldn't make out anyone's names. But as performers were eliminated, you could begin to hear audience members shouting out, "Simone Biles" or "Sasha and Normani!" My favorite, of course, was, "Rashad and Emma!"

I knew that the evening was going to be a challenge emotionally, but I wasn't prepared for what I had to watch just moments before we danced. Emma and I were already standing on our marks, the spot where we'd each begin the dance, but the backstory to our dance was being broadcast in the studio for the audience.

In preparation for the show, DWTS had sent a film crew to my parents' new home in Forest, Virginia, to interview them. The show broadcasted that reel, which included my brother Bryan, as well as interviews they'd done with Emma and me.

After watching ten seconds of it, I whispered to Emma, "I don't know if I'm gonna make it."

In the short clip, I admitted that while I was growing up I'd felt so alone because my dad and I weren't close. But I also explained, "My dad gave up his life for his family, and I felt, in college, that it was my time to give up my dream for him." When Mom shared that part of our journey on camera, both she and Dad broke down crying. Then I explained, "2006 was my most memorable year because that's when I began to realize what unconditional love means."

Before we stepped out on stage, Emma and I both wiped tears away. She gave my hand a squeeze to remind me that I wasn't alone.

I wish that everyone could feel what I felt during that dance. It was the first dance of the season that I wasn't thinking about my next move. Everything about it just flowed, and I felt like I was painting a picture and not dancing. The choreography began by showing me longing for my father's love. The moves depicted me leaving again and again, but always returning in search of that love. Toward the end of the song, I cradled Emma in my arms and at that point we—meaning my father and me—reversed roles. The whole dance unfolded to symbolize each of us giving and receiving unconditional love. Emma had put together such a beautiful expression of our story, and performing what she'd created felt effortless.

When the dance ended, I ran over to my father, who was seated beside Mom in the front row of the audience. I fell to my knees and wrapped my arms around him. Both of us were bawling like babies, and that was just fine. (I heard that even the judges were crying!)

That evening, I was the first star of the season to receive a ten from any judge up to that point. And after nine years on the show, it was Emma's first time ever receiving a ten as well. Honestly, that was one of the special things about our partnership: we were both rooting for each other to win just as much as ourselves.

While I wasn't aware, in that moment, of how other people were reacting to the performance, I realized later that it had touched so many because so many could relate to that deep, primal yearning for unconditional love. My hope then and today was that our dance would inspire those who saw it to better appreciate the relationships they have with those they love and to know that a family that prays together truly does stay together.

Wrap

After the show, my family went out to eat at the Cheesecake Factory. Butch was there, and Bryan and Pam came too. Even Pam's brother Maurice—my childhood best friend (whose son is also my godson)—was with us! I couldn't have asked for anything more. We shared a great meal and had lots of laughs together that night.

My family always gets a kick out of people's reactions to me in public. They love the opportunity to help make a fan's day. If they see someone who appears to be a fan but is afraid to approach, they jump at the chance to usher them over for an introduction and picture. And of course, I never refuse because it's an incredible gift to be able to make a moment in somebody's day extra special. I do not take it for granted. (Again, there's nothing special about me—it's the position.)

No matter what, my family sees me as the same old Shad. But that particular night, as folks walked by and whispered or asked for selfies or autographs, all the attention gave my family the giggles.

Before we left the restaurant, I bent down to give Dad a hug good-bye. His eyes were locked on mine, and they sparkled with gratitude.

"Shad," he said, "I'm proud of you."

After our fabulous evening, Butch came back to my apartment and we stayed up late talking.

Butch admitted that when our dad's health failed, he felt bitter about it—like he'd lost both a dad and a mom in the chaos of that time. But Butch also noted that he'd seen me handle that situation differently than he had. Instead of pulling back, I dove in. At the time, I remember trying to coax Butch into connecting with our dad, encouraging him, "Just call him! Tell him a joke! He'll love it." But my pep talks hadn't been enough to change Butch's heart. As we all do sometimes, he needed something more. He needed an opportunity to *feel* it.

That night, Butch felt it. He shared that the story that Emma and I had told in the dance connected to something deep inside him. He'd seen our dad appreciated, and he felt it deeply.

"Shad," he admitted, "you made me look at Dad through a different lens tonight."

That, an expression of appreciation from the man who'd mentored me in our father's absence, was the crowning moment of one of the most special nights of my life.

Unconditionally

The lyrics to Katy Perry's "Unconditionally" are about loving someone as they are—good days and bad days. It is still such an important song to me as I think about my life and my relationship with my dad.

When I was 13 years old, I made a vow that I was not going make the same choices as Dad when I grew up: smoking, drinking, and embracing bitterness. *If* I never had that really painful conversation with him, I might have ended up being someone very different than the person am. That decision quite possibly saved my life, and in a way, it saved my dad's life too. Being loved unconditionally changed his heart, and allowed him to finally express his love for me and others.

As a 13 old, I was dealing with poor physical health, my father's emotional absence, and learning challenges. But in the midst of those obstacles, I knew that the One who did love me unconditionally was walking through the storms with me. God had my back and has always been the One guiding me through the *if* moments in my life.

I'm aware that the challenges and opportunities you are facing, and will face, are unique. Even if our stories have similarities, your journey belongs to you. That's why I really want you to hear that you are not alone. You are known and loved. You are treasured by God. And I'm convinced that *if* you're committed to making the most of this life you've been given, you have everything you need to succeed.

That's not to say that success will be easy. I can testify that it's not! Succeeding at what you put your mind to will require commitment and determination. But I do believe that when you chase after a dream, you can realize it by trusting God, working hard, believing in yourself, finding the support you need, and making decisions that will help you achieve your goal.

Today, can you see where you want to be 12 months from now, or in three years, or ten years? Can you visualize yourself living successfully? Once you can see the end game, begin to visualize how you want to get there. Then, step by step, make choices that are right—right for you, right for your future, right for the people you love, right for your community. You have the chance to accomplish incredible things *if* you allow yourself to dream. Those dreams for the future—and the confidence you have in them—will guide you to success.

CONCLUSION

Remember how I rocked the "dirty bird" dance when I was a kid? As a player in the league, I developed my own touchdown celebration. When I release the ball, I use both hands to trace the outline of a double doorway in front of me. Then I open those doors and slide on through!

To me, that image represents the countless opportunities I've been given, as well as those I'll continue to pursue. And although I have no idea what doors will open down the road, I know that I'll always be ready to walk through them.

I've been best known for my performances on the field and on the stage, but one of the initiatives I'm most excited about these days is building out my philanthropic ventures. I've partnered with Awl & Sundry to create a custom luxury shoe line, and for every pair that is sold, a pair of shoes is donated to a schoolchild in Kenya who is in need. I've also continued to expand the Rashad Jennings Foundation. With the help of a lot of people, we're investing in the Lynchburg community through our 80 Weekend fundraiser, Camp 180, and Family Fun Fest. We're also impacting the lives of kids across the country to raise up the next generation of successful leaders. Through our Locker Room Project/Reading Challenge in schools around the country, by training and mentoring young athletes, and by promoting exercise and healthy diets, we're investing in children and inspiring them toward success.

Last, but not least, I've gotta say, one of the coolest and most meaningful experiences I've had happened in 2017. A kid who once rocked a 0.6 high school GPA was invited to give the commencement address at Liberty University to over 10,000 people. (No pressure!) Let's just say it took me longer to agree to that one than it did to commit to *Dancing with the Stars*! If you're wondering how it went, I can tell you that my inspirational address to the graduating seniors *did* involve pyrotechnics. So, yeah, it went well.

While there are so many amazing things happening in my life, I'm always looking for more of those doors to open. So . . . what's next for me? Lately, I've been dabbling with acting, guest-starring on a few shows. I love the challenge of creating a character, and I consider acting a form of poetry. I'd even love to write my own scripts: I already have notebooks filled with scenes and dialogue for a romantic comedy. And you know I have the soundtrack picked out, so stay tuned!

I eventually want to be trained as a marriage counselor,

and I'm also interested in being licensed as a football agent. Who better to represent players than someone who's been there? I'd love the opportunity to secure the best contracts for players, and I also want to invest in them, the way my brothers invested in me. My goal would be to help athletes make the best choices they can for their lives and their families during and after professional football.

While I can't yet see what's on the other side of every doorway I'll encounter, I do know the One who is guiding me as I take those steps. God has always been there for me, and I have every confidence that God is leading me today. As I look back over the life I've lived thus far, I recognize God's face and hand and voice in each of the pivotal *if* moments of my journey.

My prayer for you is that you will develop eyes to recognize the *if* moments in *your* life. It's important to remember that most of them will be small moments. They will be those little choices that you make in the rhythm of your everyday life. *Will I order a side of fries or carrots? Will I sprint those last ten yards? Will I volunteer on Saturday? Will I stay up an extra hour to finish my chemistry homework? Will I have the guts to persuade an employer to hire me? Will I choose to be like my dad? Will I say something that's hard in this conversation that needs to be said?* While it's easy enough to minimize these daily encounters, these are the *if*s that determine the contour of the life you'll live, beginning today.

The good news is that the *if* in life isn't up to someone

else. It's up to you! And the even better news is that the One who made you and loves you the most has your back. He is with you every step of the way.

It's time to get off the sideline, and into the end zone. You got this!

Rashad

Educator guide available for download at

http://TheIfInLifeBook.com/

ACKNOWLEDGMENTS

I could literally fill the next few pages with thanks to people who in some way, shape, or form, have been a part of helping me become the man I am today. But that wouldn't be practical. So I've relegated my acknowledgments to those people in my life who have directly helped in the production of my first-ever published book.

Thank you, first and foremost, to my Lord and Savior, Jesus Christ, without whom I could do nothing. Secondly, I want to thank my immediate family for jumping through all kinds of short-notice hoops to help me collect all the information I needed to retrace the steps of my life. Momma Jennings! I thank you for being my rock. I know that I can always depend on you. Much thanks to you, too, Pops! You encourage me to go for my dreams and to know that no matter the outcome of my efforts, you will always be proud of me. Special thanks to my brothers, Bryan and Butch. You both continue to be my inspiration. Not only could I not have made it through high school without you, I wouldn't have recalled half of my high school information for this book without you. I am proud to have you as my brothers!

To Margo Starbuck, I give a tremendous THANK YOU! As busy as my life is, I simply could not have completed this 50,000 plus word project without the amazing assistance of the superbly talented writer and visionary that you are.

A special thanks to Keith Bell, my friend, mentor, and the project manager for this book: you must have read it through ten times during the writing process! I truly appreciate you, man!

I would also like to thank my amazing friend, Christina Hovestadt, who did outstanding legwork to get the original proposal to Zondervan, I say from the bottom of my heart, thank you so much!

Thanks also to the outstanding support of my agent, Jennifer Keene, and Octagon, for your excellent service in handling all the contractual aspects of this extremely important project.

And finally, I want to thank Zondervan, for being willing to help me share my story with the world.